Hallmark

Other books by Emily Isaacson:

Little Bird's Song

Voetelle

The Fleur-de-lis

Hours From A Convent

Ignatia

House of Rain

Snowflake Princess

A Familiar Shore

City of Roses

Victoriana

The Blossom Jar

Hallmark

Canada's 150 Year Anniversary

Emily Isaacson

Published in the United States by Dove Christian Publishers, an
imprint of Kingdom Christian Enterprises, Bladensburg, Maryland.

ISBN 978-09986690-3-8

Library of Congress Control Number: 2017956468

Cover design: Voetelle Art & Design
Cover image © Szabolcs Szekerem.
License X Fotolia.

The Wild Lily Institute
P.O. Box 3366
Mission, B.C. Canada
V2V 4J5
www.wildlilyinstitute.com

Dedicated to Sophie Grégoire-Trudeau

Be not offended:
I speak not in absolute fear of you.
I think our country sinks beneath the yoke;
It weeps, it bleeds, and each new day a gash
Is added to her wounds . . .

—William Shakespeare

The parliamentary
complex
was formally opened
with a grand ball held by
the Governor General,
Lord Dufferin.
Carriage
after carriage arrived
on the spring evening of
March 27, 1876,
and fifteen hundred guests,
gaily appareled in costumes
of every imaginable sort
were received.

—Emily Isaacson, The Fleur-de-lis

Contents

Section I: Stand at the Window

for books are opened, like windows,
to worlds . . .
          —Emily Isaacson

Part One: Dogwood Manor

Dogwood Crest

Lulla-lu, there is a voice here.
Lullaby-lu, a child sighing,
the wind is crying,
the fairies hide, dear.

Lulla-lu tiny child,
you open your small hands,
your eyes are wider to lands.
Lullaby-lu, slumber mild.

Your basket swings under the dogwood tree,
the flowers open to cradle the new,
and beloved generations before you,
their fragrance encircles me.

You are a lamb in the peppermint,
wooly-girl, a docent to the gallery
of books, in a field encircled by trees,
the grass and herb leaves glint.

All are loved within this circle of trees,
sanctity is royal navy,
and marriage is fit for a lady,
redeemed to loyalties.

Lulla-lu, but rest in sleep,
now off to the lullaby world
said your mother's curls,
before the shadows creep,
before the branches weep.

Threnody of the Thistle

Thistle manor, away off the moor,
here the thistle down blows . . .
and away lullaby, mother sing,
lullaby to a prince and a king.
Here there is no sense of repeat,
just a mild prickly pod bed,
enumerating the signs
of harvest to summer's end.
The trees and the heather
all lean like the wind.

Eventually the thistle down speaks—
down, down, thistle moor,
dusting o'er the creaking floor
to the stone gorse garden door:
resurgence from poverty to kin,
from ignorance to education,
forgiving liniment
from within, cold without
from the imminent
moor fog, hazing our sight.
From cradle to Yule log,
burn foolish, burn bright!

Woman Prophet

The quiet twilight
stole your mail,
and unshod,
your peace disturbed,
from wanton crest.

The hill country
laid down
its arms,
and minstrels
now stood
in sudden malady,
a plate of victuals
not their own.

A sacred innocence,
and small dove-light tunic,
from a moment waylaid
in the mountains of the sun.

Where I Found Her

I found her
in a woodland meadow,
crafting a piper's tune,
the village brushed and eyes apart,
we, Sir,
beleaguered and bled
injustice.

He was tall without a hunch,
the castle on the moor,
echoed in glass,
the cottage thatch and thrush,
a recall
to Notre Dame's vast naves.

In this meadow,
the goldenrod,
crackling underfoot,
the sky a stormy
chase of thunder . . .
She stands,
two immigrants
in sorrow at the task
of Scotland, shapely
in a coat of arms.

Spiritual Touch

The touch of a king
would condescend to heal;
if one was touched
one hundred times,
one would turn into a princess.

If you had loved
so dearly, the beloved:
the early sky, a dark jewel
in domes of foreign temples.

Their hands clasped,
knees tightly bent,
a burning sword
thrust between
the mind and soul;
and the deepened heart
will arise in the splendor
of modesty.

One million children
stand at the gates
of their straw village,
asking to be let through:
to where the golden bird
welcomes dawn,
the translucent orb of sun-star
crossing the sky
from morning to sunset;
I tend my mantra of gardens
just before dusk . . .

The glass of time, so fragile,
and cloven antelope hooves
upon the sand:
tidings meant to clothe despair with
purity, the oils of acacia
and eucalyptus.

Glassy water
in the riverbed, too dry;
the speaking of the white raven,
and unheard silence:
my memorized word
so clear and vibrant—
to a diseased room.

What enchantment
shall I break to heal you?
O ebony soul, caught within
the prisons of deformity
and the sepulcher
of infertility and pain:
Peace.

The kiss of wisdom
is a touch piece,
and the dying,
healed do ascend.

A Gift With Outstretched Hands

I give you the land of Canada,
the gifts of following further,
growing in silence,
and daring to believe in beauty.

This country emerges from
its wintry love
to become warm with reconciliation;
we are witnessing of change.

Canada, expanse
of the beautiful and free,
may liberty crown you with justice
in the realm of the unseen.

Called out of the dust of time,
you are a dramatic child who began
as you swelled beneath
your mother's heart.

The birth pains have
made you the country you are today,
as strong as you are wide, multi-cultural,
and a captured mosaic.

Israel, we grant you amnesty
within the borders of our nation,
within our anthem,
our indivisible faiths
in restoration.

A New Valley

While I was waiting here,
he conducted the symphony:
his head was wreathed in clouds,
he had climbed a mountain
and the air was thin, but there
was a message for him at the top.

He spoke of new beginnings,
a time for children to be born,
to be rosy-cheeked with health;
a time to plant the fields,
a time for new ideas,
and countries to be made over.

I bought a lavender farm:
its fragrance rolled off into the sunset,
I was emaciated
with reckoning, afraid to live
and unprepared to die,
unsure how to continue.

This is a new vein—
being extravagant, healing souls
with rough flowers,
gathering the bitters in linen,
now that the fear is over,
when we reach a summit
and dare not go on alone.

Holding hands is new oil
that flows through the valley
of San Jacinto,
where I dream and you speak:
the oratorio glistens with wealth—
of thoughts and revelation.

Part Two: Inform the World

Time for a Poet

I would be born a poet in a coat,
I keep this letter to you in my pocket, casting
you, I will give it to you in time lasting,
although I would rather milk the goat.
I've lived a thousand years, in league with tea,
I drink in more and more of earth's light,
with every cup, I sanction blight;
a woman who informs with words the trees.

For no one holds my hand upon the road,
I walk forever with no observant end,
am I expecting strangers or friends around the bend?
and heavy-lidded is the horse's load.
He plods with cares I could not comprehend,
even and staid, I hold his mane,
he eats his oats and keeps me sane,
a horse's nature I would recommend.

There is a hill I lingered on,
fast as the light was fading low,
the moon had almost risen through night's blow,
into the future I gazed long.
A creator could not lie beneath the ground,
she would fly away—a solemn bird,
or insist years later on being heard,
her voice would, as seas, unrelentless pound.

Her old thick voice would be an ancient roar
of blood beneath the ground that fed the roots
of heavy trees with their dusky fruit,
grapes would cry at winepress upon the floor.
It became a red wine river flowing down
to an oil sea, where I found a hand
extended as a moon shines o'er the land,
illuminating the first peoples' indigo crown.

It was then I could see future's subtle shape,
a rabbit disappeared into its glen,
a deer within the meadow nibbling then,
I could affix my broken wing with tape.
But slowly I die as the world peaks,
my essence ebbs away, a shrinking empire:
the verse that once sang as a carefree lyre
is now the hardwood floor that creaks.

My chest of treasures holds
mementoes of me pausing blue,
the shape-shifting need for the spirit mood
to live in a vase or some other mold.
As life bore down on me in myths,
the deepening of each ponderous basin,
the cracking of porcelain's pandemonium,
became doctors condemning wordsmiths:

They could not die, or they would rise,
they could not live, for faintness exclusive,
they breathe last breaths, hiding reclusive,
they could not pray, it would be lies.
Thus the smoke rises early and remotely,
preparing me for another day of praise,
of the war within that makes me raise
worship to its feet shyly:

It was a dead friend in a tomb sealed,
he had lain there many days as old hymns,
and now no one had eyes weeping anymore, rims
of sunken sight, when they could be healed:
I stretched out my hand,
I called our broken worship to come forth—
where we all criticised our brethren's worth,
and made him sweat and till the land.

Levites, I will be a singer if there is a song,
while wringing the last of the water
from the linens, I hum at bees' laughter,
a woman is a word-keeper all the day long.
The convent is not too far south
of this old house in the back-woods of Mission—
they might be associates of rites and confessions,
and contemplation did not need a mouth.

Renew my Wisdom

My wisdom was one of disparity
in my journey of innumerable years,
as I parted with the star-sodden
land of my youth,
I abandoned myself
in search of a new King.

City of distant lights,
I wept in your arms,
I distilled your flowering blooms
beneath the starlight,
when the far-off land beckoned,
I echoed its cry.

There is a plumage in turquoise
that lines the peacock walls of my dwelling place,
there is gold melting in my arms,
I can smell the myrrh,
and my gifts seem to have
become ancient now.

Renew me as
I am made new;
in the spirit of intimacy,
do not withhold your gifts from me.

You will be born
in a distant land,
you will be a ruler,
with new decrees
and untouched powers.

I Saw Three Ships

A cultural horn blew, and the three ships
went sailing from Spain.
It was a summer's day in the Golden Age,
and flags fluttered brightly
from the sea port.
The colourful peasants waved
as the ships left Eurasia
for the winds and coast of Africa.
Their journey was based in economics.
This fleet was followed by hundreds
of ships, all from different ports
and different harbours, transporting goods,
carpets, perfume, spices,
in the medieval days of the internet.

Sailors were superstitious at first—
could they navigate by the stars?
Their seemly ideas on shell-shaped islands, sea-lanes
and surface currents, with or without a compass—
domains and dreams all coinciding.
When there were so many ships
and ports, it could present a front
of naval disorder, a mixed basket of citrus,
but not so, and sites stayed
orderly as sea stars,
and well-arrayed as invisible jellyfish.

The sea was stormy at will,
their ship of three masts,
in insecure connections, grids,
choppy waves, overloads, and black outs
when sailors would lose cargo,
bleed wind from the sails and let out sea anchors.

Through their sectioned panes,
artists painting in the morning—
spotting the far-off lateen sails—could
only dream of what was to come,
ships, tapestries, and glittering sunrises.

This Is Where You Keep Me

I.

If I did not die young,
I would become baroque
in movement,
and emotional relevance.
I climbed a hallmark tree
within a child,
I bade her try her pen,
and not be wild as the sea.
The rolling island hills
remind me of England's
pleasant green.
The fort is aged and
crumbling, now a relic
in the sun glinting offshore.
There was one thing I
wanted to tell you:
I have written it down
on this folded piece of lined paper.
Life has not become
a busload of people,
rather eclectic,
that I don't know and haven't met.
Of course, I was
on my way to music lessons,
the cool dark interior
of a house in Oak Bay.
I would play for my
medieval teacher
something she had not heard.

II.

I have seen you all your life,
but I had not heard you before,
I did not know that you
could play with anger,
and I would notice.
You are without malice,
an African violet;
I am only a mother
and I do not have time.
Write your lessons,
and your teachers will be proud
that you are obedient,
young and strong.
Do you know where
I want you to end up:
I want you to have tea
with me when you're four
and when you're forty.
We are a tea-party of two,
and if books abound,
there is no need to write.
Just listen:
listen to the singing,
listen to the eventide's note,
the disappearing light,
and the last flown
yellow-rumped warbler.

III.

My teacher stoked the fire
of my mind,
as the flaming red curls
to her waist.
Her voice was like
Fitzgerald in the Jazz Age,
and it was liquor.
The piano was
black and smooth
beneath my touch,
inviting a cadence.
There was a woven tapestry
in the room, and it lent
acclaim to a regal woman
with a long line of students.
To try any new music,
I would have her approval
and in the era
the arts would communicate
involvement.
I wanted the church's approval
to write, but I did not ask,
or I might not have completed
a long list of things to do.
There are gate-keepers
of our inner children,
so I only asked to play
inside the black wrought-iron gate:
this is where you keep me.

IV.

You are beloved and
this is where you keep me,
I am a photo
in a locket over your heart.
I am your mother:
on summer days
you gather your picnic
with wildflowers,
and take a blanket.
It was my golden
rag-time piano that could
turn a tune,
reminding you of the roaring twenties.
This was a proper house.
I was a minister's wife,
wore a dress,
and baked pies.
There was homemade bread
from the grain
I ground,
and kept in the cold storage.
Why do I have to ensure
you are good enough
to write,
and take what comes as
a result?
You are old enough
with your pen to make your
own decisions,
somehow you'll survive
behind your own black gate.

V.

I might be only
an aspen sapling,
or I might be old now,
with glittering leaves,
and porous bones, who is to say?
The tea from long ago
is still steeping in my cup.
The dance of time
continues on,
and little girls join
with new pink shoes.
I sat at the window
for a few years,
wondering if it was a feast
or a famine.
I joined the army
and they made me head up
the Canadian military
with pomp and gunfire.
They still stand at attention,
waiting for me to be born,
while hailing in unison
a new world.
This is the Baroque period
if we have our own opinions
on corsages, buns, and bobby pins
and how it should be done with grace.
We are married again,
the reverence sounded,
we are irregular jewels.

Section II: Mottled Recession

my forehead, salted with death—
as the night fades into remnants of dreams
to endure . . .
                    —Emily Isaacson

Part One: Layered Realism

Historical Hurricane

The recession stretched for almost a decade,
as vast rooms that go on and on,
as the lucid dreams
over oak floors
temper the alpine mist.

The flamenco-red walls,
and the kaleidoscope of lights
endeared history.
Here I sit—
bold and proud as
a tartan plaid.

I could dance in an organic whole
of limbs and pauses
before the hurricane;
with a rather moody folk skirt
brushing the granite hearth.

There was only a wind at the chimney.

That would be my signature style
of delicate arches,
brilliant height,
and stony-blue curves.

What the Lilac Was Not

The lilac was not lustrous,
but rather historic,
alas, I did have to explain
each delicate trivet of colour,
each satin sheen of purple,
next to the rich plum and deep wood.

The flourishing variety of botanicals
beyond the velvet drapery,
through the meld of glass,
echoed its mystery,
a contrast to the century-old molded
plaster ceilings,
growing archaic with beauty.

Simply, the garden
unfolded through time
like a linen cloth,
with each dried flower held
in it as potpourri.

A Little Fury

It was a magical silver wood,
all glittering with the dew,
where the light gleams through morning's seams,
and fairy wings are not lack-luster,
speaking of iridescent things.

A furious thunder storm sprang up, threat-laden
from the other end of the garden,
where the hummingbirds and bumblebees
hang on florets, like tea bags in steeping tea,
sipping the drifting transient fragrance
before darting into the forest oak trees
that are solid before the fury.
The grey squirrels and the rabbits scurried,
even their young were hurried
into their burrows before the wind.

The storm haphazardly whipped
the evergreen branches root to tip,
scattering fern fronds hither and thither;
the aristocratic deer will not today delay,
though they usually in these paths meander,
drinking the nectar from flowers of clover.
The rain melted the blue and green
into rivulets pristine.

In Relevant Cards

Feeling lost in the room
of hickory-plated emotions,
where dreams could be almost trite,
there were deep roots and tall branches
of the tree of my life,
that brushed my skin
when I stopped in the card aisle.

I am too innocent
to consider that my most jaded sentiments
could be passable in a card, leisurely and soft,
with underwriters,
hope under their belts.

My anger melts like ice cream,
sweet and sticky, with chocolate chips,
drips to be caught as holidays and moments
when we can't forget to send
a wish, a note, a card . . .

Petrified Wood

There is something durable
about immortality,
the iconic style of nature—
a petite woman
in a little black dress.
She is first living and warm,
then aging:
turning from sepia browned,
to diamond-icy and dying,
then dead with journalistic starkness.

And she rises
each spring,
with her immortal cloak
of color. Dazzling gardens,
a glitz of fragrance,
shooting the crystalline rain
clear through
with sun,
bereft of fear
of her time in arrears.

Apples of Gold in Settings of Silver

When you spoke, I listened,
and it was as the pattering of rain
after a long dry spell in the Fraser Valley,
soaking the yellow ground.
There were diamonds of glassy water
like tears on the eyes
of the flat blueberry fields.
They welled up
into juicy night-blue stones,
like sapphires grow in caves
for Lady Sappho.

The baby, in her white eyelet bonnet,
sat on a blanket in the afternoon.
She was the muse of time
and the canyons of her ears
heard the songs of the rivers and the forests;
we painted her that day
on cardboard,
as we could not afford a canvas.

Reservoir Blue

The potter's wheel turned around and around,
lassitude becoming pottery
from deep within the ground.
Clay being tamed and pulled
from a wild blue coal:
fierce and swift, to re-worked, reserved,
light over the sea, conserved.

This sentimental molding is making you resent
being rather old-fashioned,
the subtle blue glaze to wet rock rationed.
It was traditional that you take a deep dive
into colour's blood,
there were the jewel tones, rather serene linens,
hanging stars in a dark wood.

I am of beauty and all she holds captive,
you said—
must I explain this prolific art
of turning 'round and 'round as a thousand earths.

Breathing Space

Where the robin red-breast made its nest,
there was a sweeping fence
overhung with subtle evergreen trees
beside the timeless garden of cornstalks,
spindles of beans,
and square strawberry leaves.

Here, in heaven
there is a window to our little earth,
where, peering through the glass
we see quite clearly—
The old steeple bells ring with song
to the purple ground
and the royalty of the wood—
this artist's green
subdued the spider's finite threads
with a crack of rain chenille.
Then the layered reparation
of old and new,
like oldest leaf clung
to newest bloom.

View of Mount Song

Did love the 'morrow break,
when winter came too fast to me,
and seeped under the door,
a mist rose o'er the woolen floor,
too fast held tightly to my feet,
and bound them.

All weighing in my despair,
I lost my soulful child there,
all hurried in the straw street.
The wind passed by
the ashen flower box and swept it nigh,
camellias to a fiery finish.

What of comfort here in the Orient,
a far away land of copper hands and lotus flowers.
A wall surrounds my heart, my days
have all been lost in a maze
of rice fields, cries ringing out from dawn, I sing
only in the dark amid burning embers on the lawn.

I am far away, too hot to touch, too alone to stay.
The sun is a round red circle in white sky.
My books are scattered in a nomad pile.
I wrote to you in burnt sienna style.

I am neither poor nor rich.
I am neither young nor old.
I am neither black nor white.
I am neither slave nor free.

In the Custody of Angels

I stood here for quite some time
with my back to you,
I was an ancient sky
decorated with only the sunrise,
and the smoke curled from the chimney
rather like the curls on your neck.

I took my angel wings and rose
from the place of a wood stove,
a fire table, and a poet
in a cabin by the river.
The clouds reflected my appearance
and equivocal disappearance.

Once I knew you quite well
and I thought you would never leave me.
I only know now that if you fly away
I'll fly away too:
the nocturne thrush twittered
on a branch just outside the clematis fence.

Beyond your prison you could see the sky
of my custodian.
You are in the custody of an angel.
She is bright, flashing and you
water-coloured her world—
just so from aged.

Part Two: Spare Minimalism

Beside the Golden Door

"Give me your tired, your poor,
your huddled masses yearning to breathe free,
The wretched refuse of your teeming shore,
Send these, the homeless, tempest-tossed, to me:
I lift my lamp beside the golden door."

— Emma Lazarus, 1883

I had not been afraid of the dark for a long time now.
My father was once scrambling eggs in bacon grease;
life was not for the faint. Everything becomes ashes.
It's not a real job unless you get your hands dirty . . .

This all started back during the recession in Canada,
a time something like the Great Depression.
People could not even afford to feed their children
and they would send them to school hungry.
Drive until you can drive no more . . .

To even turn away a glass of milk
was considered ungrateful.
You said thank you to God at every meal.
Your eyes are wide open.
You can't do this job and be soft . . .

Rival, you stopped telling fairy tales for once
and admitted you were short on dimes—
that is why you stand in the street.
You are singing, though, a song in time gone by.
Stand, until your bones ache with exhaustion . . .
Brother, can you spare a dime?

A Second June

Survivalist, how deep is the wound?
There is a second sun, a second June,
disparate over the terrace
where golfers play seraphs
after the first iced-tea afternoon.

This is the letter to my second wind,
where I rename myself Canadian;
eloquent islanders travel the roads within,
and paint the world by re-framing.

Poverty causes angst among martyrs,
among the once wealthy—
selling the rings of their former partners,
what people will do for money.

What people will do out of desperation
tells something of their ruffled character feathers,
and newspapers have absconded restoration—
they have fallen on hard times and rainy weather.

A Street of Many Doors

There was a row of doors,
each different, speaking like the mouth of a house
as they opened and shut,
whereby the words could come in and go out.

There was the ornamental screen door on each,
white, brown, black, red, framing the entrance
while citizens of Mission City sat on their porches:
one old plaid woman in a rocking chair,
a young guy with long hair, strumming
his silver-stringed banjo.

Fleur was the little woman;
she stood at the gate to the garden at dusk,
the fragrance rose and cracked,
the petals were like the folds of her dress.
"We love our house," she said.
"Our house has deep shadows;
the shadows of saying hello
and the shadows of saying goodbye."

I climbed on my delivery bike with its basket
and rode through the street all night
with the downtown newspapers.
They were folded like origami.
By five, it was early morning,
and the sun was just beginning to rise.
I was standing in the street in ripped jeans;
it beheld my sackcloth as a fierce tiger lily.

A Third April

The third time the spring came in
she wore Laura Ashley with hues of mint,
a dash of thyme, that friend of mine,
and a hat with a hint of velvet.

She hung a flower on the wood wall,
and many more irises appeared
in purple and orange, the brightest color
under the ten commandments.
Moses would engrave
your name
in a leather-bound Bible.

What prophet would I ask
to interpret the recession
and the subsequent poverty:
Moses or Samuel?
The next door neighbor lost his job,
his daughter joined a homeless camp,
my grandmother's second husband died
of pneumonia,
my father could not leave a tip,
while I bought even more irises than before.

A House of Many Walls

The tall Mission windows, where time and distance meet,
looked out over the populace passing by in the street;
I placed two glass lanterns with flues on two lamp stands.
Then I filled them with olive oil from Israel's last strands
echoing down the Mount of Olives.

The lamps burned through the day and into the night
lighting a lofty perch of dizzying height
where my wood ladder reached
almost to the ceiling roses and plaster cornices,
against the stacks of books in all languages, all colours,
and there were bookmarks emboldening the quotes
from the holly hedgerow.

She grows in orderly descant on Cemetery Road,
a tiny woman in green becomes this bed of thorns,
and renaissance from the inkwell flows
while the morning's dew each grave adorns.

There were thin walls in this old house of herbs,
the opaque cups filled with boiling water curbed
the taste for anything but tea: rich, deep, and smooth;
the doors opened when the flood of customers came through,
laughing in a myriad of colors, that they had found you.

Now the blue glass glows at even bright,
one tall pillar candle burns steadily—though the night,
the beeswax emits its character light in shallows dulcet,
burning the candle at both ends and two hemispheres met;
no one could accuse you in your coldness of going South.

When the winter comes, you'll be miles ahead
with the camomile for all those fallen ill in bed.

In the Pauper's Mine

I—in my grave,
and death wandering over me,
wondering where I went.
If I was even remotely clever,
I would be there still.

There was a tall hill where death lived,
and he struck out at night,
looking for rather unwanted
or wanton individuals,
looking for scrap iron.

The miner left to work in a pauper's mine,
his apple slices browned,
there were no gems in the ceiling,
there were no wine glasses with tall stems,
just the draughts and the dark.

I had buried gold under the cedar, and he dug it up.
What would he do with a lace doily?
Why would he trace its quiet pattern?
The table was old, as the oil in the olive hills,
and the missionaries left for Mount Song.

"Cheep, cheep," said the yellow canary—
she was ready to die if need be,
with a soft molten lava heart,
fluttering in the chickweed.

Nothing free is ever cheap.
Nothing cheap is ever free.

What We Found Over Breakfast

By candlelight I pen this solemn note,
to the master and the mistress of this house,
I am no bigger than a field mouse,
but I have sailed upon the seven seas,
and now—what has become of me—
I cannot speak for misery—

It was in a moment of charm
that I accepted the old house with open arms.
This burned-down house—
the morning finds but none too soon—
was charred by my own match;
a fiddler's tune I played upon the thatch,
your rooftop bearing me, it let me stay,
but now that mournful resonance
is but insoluble dissonance.

If I should run from you
I must confess
that it was I who fell from grace
with just one note—
upon your blackened cinders
grand old house, I stand,
with now an inextinguished hand.

With terror, I would flee
into the night—
I would desist from digging at the site
of one more grave—
the Esplanade—
a place that once was loved
lies in unbeguiling ashes
not caused by anyone excepting me.

A coward, I would bow
to take my strap—
I would stretch out my hand
at curt command
but would the haunting eyes
that looked out o'er the plains
be no more furious distain.

Sky Wreath

Where the ivy tresses curl on the brick wall
beyond the cream sashes,
how do I remark of the browned landscape,
why would I reveal its bitter heritage—
a line of leafless maples—
its well of blood,
its bruised remnants, covered with snow,
its silvered pencil scratching for liberty . . .

And the minions of earth conceal
the frozen swans in black gloves
at season's wintry white,
the buoyant spice with cloven antlers
in heated ion discourse,
and why four apples and the tiny round cardamom
munitions swim darkly, hidden in the cider,
when the early indifferent smoke
from the chimney wreaths the sky.

Dreamscape Gray

Handsome, my sepulchral lot,
to lie within a churchyard plot,
to close my eyes in morbid air,
there is nothing I take with me there—
beneath the old ash tree.

My eyelids are now sealed forever,
no more to flutter—just encounter—
spirits of a better kind,
sojourned to my pallid mind.

I have died from sea to sea,
where I cried with morning's icy throng
and evening's tea.

There was a tear
that fell into my cup;
no more to handle,
I have lived enough.

My Little Black Book

In search of stones
to adorn the graves of those I have left behind—
it is true, you were once a friend,
now I can only mourn you
as a sweet wind mourns the pines,
for once you were very present in me,
and I could not forget your preferences
in music and in lunch, out-of-the-way haunts,
they were paramount to our keeping,
the bonding crafts that kept our hands busy.

I thought today, perhaps if I send you this note,
you will remember the good times we have had,
the griefs we have forgotten,
and take me out of the cupboard of your heart,
dust me off, and revive me.

Part Three: Gothic Architecture

The Peace Tower

The monumental space,
inlaid floor and
glorious chandelier,
ornamental gold
and stained glass windows;
cross row,
one verse of plume
upon your epitaph,
one marble center
of the Saint Laurent
to seam the last
velvet seam—
brocaded walls,
art adorned,
stacked several stories deep
in the canticles of law.

Where the Royal William Rose lingers
along the manicured walk,
and eyes grow bright at
the last half-door,
a corridor to the
heart of the
commons room.

The Little Match Girl

In the dark, a little girl in a cotton shawl
struck a match to keep warm.
It illumined the stone structure
of the Peace Tower she leaned against,
the gargoyles against the night sky.
Gothic architecture
reaching almost to heaven
stretched its lacy fingers,
blotting the stars with its handkerchief—
its rhetorical icons
simmering prayers in the shadows.

There was a patchwork quilt
of nations, that had grown faded
with the rain and snow,
of the many colours of skin
that made up the face of a country,
of the many films from the National Film Board.

A match box was ten cents;
a passerby gave her a dime
as she stood in the gutter,
and she collected them in her apron.

Anna Pavlova

Set IV

One plié is
exactement
seul—
and alone you will
face them,
alone, you will
dance.

Set V

Giselle is you,
Anna, and in your
shoes are the
feet of worlds,
unannounced.

Riveting—
sparkling in the spools
of splendor: an ode to
the fairyland wedding,
gift by gift.

Ara

I.

The sacred mind, of virtue and its
innocence, the small white lamb
on the altar of sacrament, and one
wistful thought, that life in all its beauty
did not disappear as a fading wind.
We thought of the times we
had spent sprawled on the lawn
before the mighty cornfield, row upon row,
drinking our iced tea, over poetry,
with biscuits and sandwiches. Until the fall, when
the desolate cornfield was ploughed into the ground.

What was too fragile to hold on, the wing
of a clay butterfly in flight was love,
ponderous and riveting, hungry, bold—
taking a canvas by surprise without
paint or artist, just a smash of glass parts
doubling back on all that was victory,
jubilee of visions casting shadows
that extended far into the parking
lot of a garden you would pay to see.
The gravedigger came by with a shovel,
faulted me on leaving a single rose.

Maria Model

It was a clear night in Toronto.
The moon shone unto the wood floorboards
like a delicate child attempting a waltz.
The young Madonna cleared her throat,
and the canvas paused,
the brush stroking her finery back into position.
The water faucet trickled—
some water for her head, her face,
even the array of plants
created an oasis against the darkwood.
Now violet and watery,
her eyes glanced about, turning into huge rims.

Astor, in his eloquence, the loft his backdrop,
struck a medieval chord—
he painted on canvas
the Sainte Maria model,
but a street woman with long mahogany hair,
who stood on the corner.
Under a lamppost it worked
exceedingly well in moonlight,
so he lit a candle in the window
and kept her up all night.
Straight and tall, she reeled,
orchestral and divine, and
his mother's dress did nothing
to faze her simplicity.

Bootes

I.

The suffering induced by the bear driver
that had seemingly no solace,
dark night of the soul,
the point of no return would take me captive.
Even so, there remained the beauty of darkness
interspersed by a radiant navy.
There was an ethereal light around the streetlamps.
I walked home from the train station.
I began to hum Barber's Overture.
I pulled my rabbit fur hood closer
around my face, and my eyelashes froze.

What was my character's resolution?
The unquiet was bronze and choleric,
the open space replaced by horses and carriages,
old roads, and stores with forged business.
I bathe drenched in the rain,
I ask for meaning when there is none;
the water streams down my hair,
outspoken that we are natural beings
marked by time and the passion of gods:
nourished to a science
and not without fruits and flowers.

Braithwaite

Aurias, on a glassy moor,
like spikenard, clutching to the bridle,
in full gallop, crossbow
and arrows in her quiver,
toward the moon-land shadowed tower.

The old wizard grafted several shoots,
in ancient looms, his tapestry grew,
jaded, royal, midnight.

Round the turn, the highwayman flew,
the honey from his tree, so sweet:
like milk and flowing lavender.

The masked crusader on his ebony horse,
his whip lay silent in its pouch,
the rushes by the river Silvermere.

One candle in the waxen bower,
the panes reflect her ivory stare,
the winter tower held her, brick by brick.

Her hair, like tresses to the floor,
white dress encircled with a crown,
her auburn, gathered 'neath the moon,
the stones of Kebar round about her.

From the mossy stone, enchantment grew,
the thunders of the willowers home,
their wildflowers, wreathed in velvet,
chants of lyre, concentric hymn,
the young and humble, sober, reunited.

The drawbridge bore them in refrain,
safe and mild, from many a mile:
wined and danced, well learned and bred,
sandaled, cloaked in godhood.

The knights around the castle bore thee,
valiant armor, fiery burgundy;
the green of pine, still in thy boughs,
the pleated wood, still innocent of thy cause,
though grief enclosed thee.

Silent moat, as dung upon the ocean,
strewn wee with golden grass and yule betiding,
the clip-clop of thy stable finery shod:
trod even, shipshape, upon the world's vast mast
at the rampart of thine heart, Eternal Rose.

Little lamb, bleating, on the pasture;
in lichen tea, your simple battles soothed.

Dorado

I.

Airy and ethereal as the wind that moves
the cocoa field, patterning the chocolate beans,
pitted against her own mortality,
the woman rises to the challenge
of each new day, singing
arias in color
through the silence
of the paned glass,
slanted rite of sunlight—
a medium of rays
that once belonged to me: as gods.

When I enter a room
I take note of whose it is,
the owner of these stunning
brights and darknesses,
and to whom everything belongs,
for this person is my thesis of the hour,
and the contrasting ideas of white on white
divine, create a hundred sonnets
where the stakes are drawn
between hell and purgatory,
between heaven and the look of two people.

The Writer's Neck of the Woods

I walked until I found one small sacred glen
where light from the sky was shaded by one still
mossy tree, blinking through this shadow world, kin
to all enchanted fairy meadow whirl, I took one quill
to note the moment's verse, still unbeknownst at
this late hour, and those who tell the time shall spy
upon the imperative, their goodly cry.

I braided my hair by the window this night
while watching the owls rise into the trees, pure
snowy white, eyes blinking soberly at light
from each planet, star and moon, festooned demure
to hang in navy-black seas of stormy might,
the ships dip in the waves of mystic cursive
where I scribbled down each last thought within sight.

Oh here, by this small book where ink meets the line
of page, and sorrow meets joy, and humour, mirth—
come with me in this final hour, the world mine,
and find the journey home, the land uncursed
where spirit meets the soul of man and reads last,
his lantern lit over the tome, the ghost
no fancy of the literate mind, here glass.

Gemini

I.

In unity we are inseparable,
indissoluble, indivisible: the cream baby's breath,
whispering a prayer for the devout.
The meter of tones and semitones,
iron and clay,
strong and regimented paired with healing.
A wreath of balsam, berries sequential,
and nature bows its burnished head
with bureaucratic respect
to institute some deeper sacrifice
than dark and the beauty of oil—then death.

I rise again.
I am a candle.
I am one million burning
before the year is through—burning in the windows,
lit because this country will not be ruled
by fluorescence.
Light a candle in the Old World
by the wailing wall,
shield it from the wind.
So they lit candles
in beeswax, soy, and paraffin.

Part Four: The Enamoured Romantic

Ace

When it snows,
I lie beneath the snow so softly
for I am of a dead and dying world.

The piece that has taken
the princess from her chamber
and cast her into the street,
she being unduly victimized,
and chanted how we chanted.

Remnant

The in and out of a door closed
in the convent of St. Clare,
a clear and vestal melody,
and heart unopened, sealed.

The Assisi dome's echoing nave,
the basilica, a mighty monument to freedom,
the thatched roof and poor hearth,
a dissident league away.

The beautiful banquet, set,
the fire of a heart without reprise—
to find a kiss,
just close your eyes.

One Still Fertile Field

Poland, 1942.
Bird against the barbed wire fence:
its faded feathers fall like snow
its voice no longer sings . . .

My naked head, bent beneath
this scarlet sky, one fast-flown prayer;
the clouds draw on, collect their rain
in thundering gray.

Ashes drift, floating through
the acrid haze,
dull the ground,
embittered, cracked,
by winter's icy frost.

I stand against the shelter
of my hope:
of youth's once salient strength—
from rat-infested rafters rings
our last unbroken cry;
and from the sky, like tears,
now falls the rain.

The freshly shoveled ground
is splattered,
watered down to mud,
but from beyond its silent seal
blood cries like thunder.

This grave of ground
beneath the snow's still sepulcher,
will hold our shattered voice
until that light
which shines beyond
eternity's door
returns to man our sight.

White sun in a black sky,
I lean into the biting wind,
I turn beneath this blood-stained moon;
I will never forget,
I cry your tears,
I hear your voices ring
beyond this earth's yet final sphere.
Why I am here and you are gone
is only pale seashells
flung
as to a raging tide.

Stars gleam beneath this gathering dusk,
sun turns to red over the sea;
what hope once burned
in me, white fire,
now rises with
the flame of night.

Cold and pure
my heart's voice sings,
and a thousand voices echo,
from a thousand souls
this freedom rings.

The Muse

Fulfill my desires to complete,
compose me, the red-haired muse until
I am half sick of shadows. Create,
make believe that I am immortal;
act—the imaginary warden,
you, real as the living blue garden.

For I am the subject, auburn bent,
of greater scrutiny than scorn rent;
I am laughter in the heart of bliss,
fairy token of the dawn's first kiss,
try me, see if I am art divine,
taste this stately dream of light confined.

What pillars rise majestic in time
of your touch upon the easel line,
what iron gate will bid you enter
to that auspicious arc of God as center,
even as we now pass in our dreams
dip each brush, and paint, within these streams.

Aria: Togetsukyo Bridge

Morning stretches its wings:
pure white light,
still in a half-dream . . .

Over the wooden slats,
footsteps ripple
sound into silence,
birds wing high,
black into the white and disappear;
waves slap sage against
the rain-gray pilings,
the windless pines wait . . .

And the mist rises with the sun,
blooming over the shoulders
of Arashiyama.

The Ship Lantern

The light on the water
gleaming at silence,
the steady hum of the prow,
and derelict rope coiled.

Where I stand, the nations wait
riveted in darkness,
fearful to trespass and
asking to eat at this fortunate table.

Where once my hair met with the wind,
and the storm in my eyes
was a virgin bow,
the sea was an unchartered course,
domain of mariners afierce.

The moon shall rise
in this salty sky,
round and full,
it will guide the way;
and the night,
flickering with candles,
will be lit by the undying
legacy of youth.

One by one, they join the stars,
perishing at the hands
of their tormentors;
death shall not overshadow
the silent song,
of what will rise
and overcome.

Constellation

We are as flowering dogwood
and Nootka rose,
planets moving
through the night
lens of milky universe,
transient as the seasons pass
without appeasement,
at the mercy of the storm.

Yet now,
I have completed
a measurable act:
I have built a home
in the wilderness,
where the beams,
warm with the smoke
of a hearth-fire,
are hung with elk
and bear,
dried sorrel and madrona;
maize and beans
dot the soup
with gold stars
in the spring sky.

Tryst

How should I know thee,
nameless, pensive,
high-bred, the ointment
of nations . . .

What priest could contend
with thy watch
and pulse, beckoning
to early paradise.

Name of the light,
I have loved thee,
watcher of the moon
and stars.

On Browning Boughs

Usher in the apple's dusk fruit over
the tread of footprints in the glen's last green,
pierced by sacred waters of dappled stream:
rain's reprisal swelling its bounds; lower
than the clouds, on wing, the feathered quail fly,
and prominent afternoon, in leather
dress, a fall hunter of the outskirts dry.

The nuthatch twitters on the browning boughs,
a nursery of tomatoes, seeded vows,
breaks red at the mountaineer's muted poem,
his stop for lodging at the farmer's home;
his knock upon the wooden frame of door,
Jack Frost, frightening his guest with white speech—
spiced inkling of a cider leaving core.

Hyacinth, handcuffed to a dying field,
the guileful cold, bereft shadow grafted,
the furrows of yesteryear, fringing yield,
the exile of vegetables, the drafted
two-tone harvest on cue, the dreamy corn;
the chestnut lookout with buckeye about
appraise the rusty treasure amid thorn.

Of Foreign Lands and People

In a torturous chair
I could speak to you,
of foreign lands and people.

My hands would explain
what is unspoken
of the domestic love
that cleans and cooks,
that mends—
of the foreclosed world,
where violence never meets
womanhood eye to eye;
the harlot neither eats nor sleeps,
and her bed is of opium.

I do ascend my secret stair,
the light, a beacon to each sea:
the night, a horse I ride to heaven,
and an angel for each wing.

The potent remedy is swung,
a sickle to the dead and dying;
we tread softly in our dreams,
in gentle poetry unsung.

Section III: Contemplative Design

Linen tapestries
the landscape,
each translucence
ripe with colour . . .

—Emily Isaacson

Part One: Velvet Statement

Home Contemplation

O true Home,
O true birth place,
O true haven or throne,
O spirit of comforting lace,
Be my reality!

O only place, at present,
Where I have decided to dwell,
(and not resent),
Be built up!

O highest aim of my maturity,
O refuge from the rain, the world and all its pain,
Shelter me!

O Subject of my present,
O Object of my future,
O Obsession with my work,
O Space between my hands and feet,
O Triune spiritual night-light,
Integrate me!

Family Contemplation

O true Family,
O true cupped hands,
O true receiver of my human humility,
O people of my home land,
Resound with purpose!

O only resonant lovers,
The mother and father who created me,
(and did not tear me down),
Be famous!

O braider of my hair, holder of the comb,
O valued members that share my home,
Visualize me!

O Subject of my breath,
O Object of my flesh,
O Relegated source of education,
O Test between nurture and nature,
O Singers of the night-time carol,
Enfold me!

Sister Contemplation

O true Sisters,
O true girlhood memoir,
O true women of my heart,
O well drawn devoir,
Sing your chorale!

O only girls with whom I share
My dreams, and let do my hair,
(and not criticize my ways),
Be praised!

O those girls who held my hand,
O sharers of my secret lands,
Validate me!

O Subject of my songs,
O Object of my strongest derision,
O Sworn keepers of the pact,
O Resting on my inner vision
O Muses of poetry vast,
Promise me!

Brother Contemplation

O true Brothers,
O true boys of my branches,
O true men of my heart's tree,
O well planted oaks,
Drivers of my soul!

O only boys with whom I share toys,
Blackberries, and mother's pies,
(and not upset my dolls and joys),
Be raised!

O those who sailed the ship's imagined veins,
O those who flew the paper airplanes,
Empathize!

O Subject of my happiness,
O Object of my gathering,
O Hunters of the deer,
O Partakers of the family meal,
O Listeners who don't grow restless,
Read me!

Ancestor Contemplation

O true Ancestors,
O true heritage of grace,
O true men and women of my colony,
O waters of my truest face,
Resurrect me!

O only line of my surviving race,
Humanity's heart beating in an open space,
(do not regret my place on earth),
Be thanked!

O ancestry of my civilian blood,
O parental call of servanthood,
Resolve!

O Subject of my long lineage,
O Object of my aim to mesh,
O Creators of my flesh,
O Hope of future children,
O Patriarchs and Matriarchs,
Look down from heaven!

Benefactor Contemplation

O true Benefactors,
O true patrons of my corporation,
O true financial foundation,
O supporters of my restoration,
Incorporate me!

O only officers of my accountability,
The ones for whom I give my all,
(and to whom I give account),
Please call!

O holistic leadership behind successful lures,
O panacea for my failure,
Ride on!

O Harness of the horse,
O Trainer of the colt,
O Mentors of my progression,
O Delineators of my succession,
O Insurers that I am an asset not a liability,
See me clearly!

Country Contemplation

O true Country,
O true place of my beginnings,
O true inviter of the alien,
O night ship's harbor,
Elucidate!

O only platform in our vulnerability,
The uniform of our individuality,
(and to whom we salute),
Our native land!

O orthodox beginning,
O true leader of a people through wilderness,
Speak our narrative!

O Place of great interior wealth,
O Grace for mystery and stealth,
O Beholder of the children's hounds,
O Keeper of the Commonwealth,
O Safety of the many peoples within your bounds,
May your borders be safe!

Land Contemplation

O true Land,
O true high mount of my citadel,
O true boundary of my worth,
O territory as long as it is wide,
Fight to defend!

O only generous benefactor,
The dimensions of our faith and of our deeds,
(and to whom we look for conscience),
Our kitchen fire!

O force to drive our law abiding,
O collaboration with the model citizen,
Seek our compliance!

O Valleys in the mist to forested peaks,
O Western plains with rodeo stud,
O Prairie fields of hard red wheat,
O Snow-cleared iced canal, and river mud,
O Territories vast to island roads last,
May your prayers be those of many faces!

Sea Contemplation

O true Sea,
O true tide of my rocky shore,
O true place where I find my soul,
O ship-wreck to those who despise you,
Salty measure of the moon!

O only diametric tide,
The didactic sea horse that does not throw its rider,
(our sandy place of peace and seashell solace),
Surge to island beaches!

O unrelenting power abiding,
O untamed are nature's depths in hiding,
Our pregnant mother!

O Seaweed turning in your underwater tryst,
O Nourishment from every krill to fish,
O Kelp upon the tide pool bares its barnacled breast,
O Pilings holding to the sand's grail,
O Terror of the ship through tempest's wail,
Our first amendment!

Sun Contemplation

O true Sun,
O true light of earth,
O true star on which we depend,
O burning peril of our atmosphere,
Source of all green life!

O only undeterred figure,
You cross the sky each day,
(and never fail to rise in precious morn),
Intellectual brightness!

O center of our solar system's mire,
O unrelenting heat in desert's fire,
An axis of greater stars!

O Farmer with his agricultural plough,
O Planter of the cultivated brow,
O Tropical jungle green heat burning bright,
O Moon and planets' father through the night,
O Strong-willed child that will not bend in flight,
All life encircles you!

Part Two: Authentic Entrance

Prayer Contemplation

O true Prayer,
O true place of lowly saints,
O true incense in a holy place,
O inner hope lifted high,
We ask for our needs!

O only unfragmented reel,
You record our organic questions,
(and don't fail to note our authenticity),
We asked for a higher power!

O central consensus of results,
O determination of our pursuit,
You are the beloved!

O Mother bird with lifted wings,
O Shield us from the snares of earth,
O Protect us from our vices and our things,
O Deliver us from desires that we birth,
O Fly in us from corruption to your resurrection,
We will not be deceived!

Meditation Contemplation

O true Meditation,
O true mindset of the peaceful,
O true kindness to one's inner self,
O reflection of our state of heart,
We see beyond the obvious!

O only repetitive practice,
Resigning my focus to the most essential,
(do I dare look away and be distracted),
There is so little concentration these days!

O I have made a plan sublime,
O I have set aside time to dive into divine,
You are the symbol kind!

O Seers unprepared for your embrace,
O Original fish net of the human race,
O Determine now our moments and our days,
O Communicate your mind to us with grace,
O I am an instrument of your music,
Retune me from within!

Vision Contemplation

O true Contemplation,
O true settling of the day,
O true vision of the anointed,
O invoking of my daily cry to thee,
Conceive me!

O only moment of understanding censured,
Bringing the incarnation of the holy nature,
(a moment when heaven touches earth),
Heaven, give us birth!

O I have eaten of an innocent tree,
O I have absconded good and evil,
You are the tree of life!

O Keep me sure-footed on the path,
O Keep my mind and heart secure with deadbolts,
O Where they cross, your crucifix or wrath,
O You are the measure of my inner revolt,
O Thank you each day for sharing your thoughts,
You are guardian of the contemplative's chamber!

Lion Contemplation

O true Lion,
O true King of Beasts,
O true stalker in the desert,
O seeker of prey,
I fear you!

O only predator who has right to hunt,
A prey that cannot him escape,
(a prayer I can't enunciate),
The pale sand speaks and roars!

O I have been consumed,
O I have forgotten your love, presumed,
You are savage!

O Keep me flying from your claws,
O Keep me rising with wings into the sky,
O You approach, it sounds, your dusty paws,
O You are the one for whom I rise,
O I relinquish my physique, torn beneath your grip,
Then I am re-knit!

Unicorn Contemplation

O true Unicorn,
O true mythical companion,
O true hidden generator,
O energy of the spirit world,
Do not bow to me!

O only co-creator,
A soft wind from your wood flute,
(a bearded whimsical),
You sell ideas in dreams!

O I have composed,
O I have felt your grip upon my throat,
You are poet to me!

O Keep me from your dangerous rage,
O You are on the mountaintop as sage,
O Keep me finding irises in watercolour,
O You are in the dark, a saviour,
O I will not detest your power,
Silvered horn!

Lamb Contemplation

O true Lamb,
O true kindness to my outstretched hand,
O true follower,
O one who lays its head beneath my crook,
Be my snowy flock!

O only copacetic,
The sound of your hooves is familiar,
(as we travel up to Oliver),
My source of sharp sheep's cheese!

O I have called you lamb,
O I have led you,
You can lie down!

O I will fight for you,
O You are on the pleasant plane,
O I have slept in dew,
O You are next to heather's flame,
O do not rest except in me,
My lovely lamb!

Shepherd Contemplation

O true Shepherd,
O true leadership in strife,
O true firm voice through the rocky night,
O one who lays it bare with toil and with sweat,
Be thou my rod and staff!

O only pastoral one,
Alone you face the rugged plain,
(the lion and the wolf are slain),
You warm yourself by firelight!

O you have called me lamb,
O you have wandered by the stars,
Your branches, kindling charred!

O I will scoop the ashes of your life,
O Olive oil, I turn the tallow into soap,
O Your lonely flute is lithe,
O Not one lamb is tied with rope,
O I shall trust your mischievous crook,
Pastoral Pan!

Lighthouse Contemplation

O true Lighthouse,
O true lamp in the storm,
O true clarity in strife,
O director of our course at sea,
Shine!

O only mediator,
Every ship thanks your light,
(the storm is abated by your power),
Brighter still!

O you have been unyielding virtue,
O diviner of the way through the dark,
Brightness!

O Beam of hope,
O Star of deepest inky black,
O Gleam of paradise,
O Not a ship before you crashed,
O You would keep us on,
Brightest!

Road Contemplation

O true Road,
O true way upon the landscape,
O true path through the unscoped wilds,
O trek over the mount of a thousand trees,
Onward!

O only highway,
Every desert is crisscrossed in pattern,
(our primitive attempts to reach oasis lands),
Forward!

O decider of the ways of humankind,
O men and women travelling through the night,
Lead on!

O You shall be raised,
O You shall rise above the trajectories,
O All beings carnal shall not overcome you,
O Your leadership is supreme,
O You arrive and depart,
Immutable clay!

Inn Contemplation

O true Inn,
O true resting place,
O true home of my home,
O water of a hundred dusty hands,
Magnify your heart!

O only home by the side of the road,
Every washbowl speaks of comfort,
(our hands and feet are cleansed anew),
Invite us!

O invitation of the open door,
O abode of people in the night,
Your hospitality!

O Yesteryears by lantern light,
O Nocturnal refuge from craggy height,
O Long plank tables piled high with food,
O Wine that lasts the night,
O Oil upon the head is poured,
We will stay!

Part Three: Signature Heartfelt Style

Mother Contemplation

O true Mother,
O true circle that surrounds,
O true love that bore,
O spirit of nourishment,
Rebirth!

O only door
into the realms of the earth and nature,
(mountain, river, and sea)
Release!

O Midwife of life and all its richness,
O Sewer of the stitched tapestry,
Order!

O Servant of the family way,
O Observer of the baby's play,
O Baker of the leavened loaf,
O Helper of the cooking fire,
O Wine of eventide is poured,
Walk last behind the child!

Father Contemplation

O true Father,
O true provider,
O true guidance,
O spirit of protection,
Teach!

O parental soul
of the child in three dimensions,
(mind, body, spirit)
Encircle!

O leader of the family home,
O covenant partner of the sacred union,
Love!

O Restorer of the cell of procreation,
O Reassurance of the universe's ordering of life,
O Strong tower, be a place of refuge
O City on a hill, now lighthouse to the ocean's roar,
O Fortress of ongoing safety amid strife,
Unify!

Elder Contemplation

O true Elder,
O true watcher of the people,
O true gain of wisdom,
O spirit of times past,
Remember!

O only illuminator
of the three dimensions of time,
(child, parent, elder)
Re-light!

O smoldering smudging burning,
O lighted flame of future vision,
Reignite!

O Sound advice from depth of night,
O Spirit of the ancient's word,
O Dreamer of the life beyond,
O Wind of legend north,
O Teacher of the ways of earth,
Redirect!

Ancient of Days Contemplation

O true Ancient of Days,
O true mountain,
O true sure-footed deer,
O sign of eternal favour,
Run!

O only cave
Where four directions blow:
(North, East, South, West)
Listen!

O day of all earth's creation bright,
O night of constellations of the heavens,
Shine!

O Prayer for deeper meaning,
O Word for understanding,
O Diviner of the nature's song,
O Highlands of the earth's vast crags,
O Diversity of senses: vision, hearing, touch, and taste,
Speak!

Daughter Contemplation

O true Daughter,
O true young singer,
O true vintage melody,
O spirit of the proverb's last word,
Intuit the rhythm!

O only receiver
of the three promises of the Divine nature,
(live, love, breathe)
Perceive life and death!

O black-haired onyx stone,
O white-haired mouth of rosehip,
Boil water o'er the fire!

O Steeping tea of herbs, infusions of the soul,
O Poultice of medicinal worth,
O Tincture of the master's hand,
O Ointment of the camphor's cool,
O Triad with the drum beat,
Reweave eternal destiny!

Son Contemplation

O true Son,
O true beat of blood in my veins,
O true bow and arrow,
O hunter of the dream world,
Find wisdom's day and night!

O only accepter
of the way things are and the way they are not,
(accept, bear, fight)
Grow courage!

O strength of my now aging bones,
O character of the courageous home,
Return to your source!

O Child of the cooking fire,
O Youth of forest's hierarchy,
O Man of hunt and gathering,
O Leader of a tribe,
O Way through the wilderness,
Set out upon the journey!

Child Contemplation

O true Child,
O true liturgy of birth,
O true song and troubadour,
O onward and inward growth,
Contemplate!

O only burgeoning invisible,
Unfolding of a flower's petal,
(respect, values, practices)
Destine!

O paradox of all forces of earth and heaven,
O irony of the sacred verse in rhyme,
Play!

O Rooted tree, deep within the ground,
O Ancient idea that breathes new life,
O Shores of endless seas within their bounds,
O Infant of the mother's breast,
O Milk of rich nourishment,
Dream!

Hero Contemplation

O true Hero,
O speaker of the play upon the stage,
O personhood we follow in renaissance,
O woman for whom we cast our vote,
Act!

O only playwright
Who wrote of protagonist before time began,
(quill, ink, papyrus)
Reach!

O landscape spanning thro the valley wide,
O heaven open to our wounded pride,
Mission of art!

O Seismic afternote from infidel,
O Music to the finest ear in perfect pitch,
O Ebony and ivory upon the keyboard of soliloquy,
O Word and verse that stands in rhyming couplet,
O Sonnet of resurrection from the past,
Great orator!

Physician Contemplation

O true Physician,
O true cure,
O true medicine,
O spirit of life and healing,
Resurrect!

O only bedside watcher through the night,
O keeper of the lantern held high
(over the miles of sick and lonely),
Revive!

O white stone hospice of the dying,
O seashell mansion of the living,
Relay!

O Prayer before a patient's final word,
O Maternal help at baby's first breath,
O Prescriber of the remedy,
O Binder of society's wound,
O Strong and wise figure tried,
Renew!

Divine Contemplation

O true Divine,
O true voice calling in the night,
O true light of day,
O spirit of saving grace,
Call me West!

O only desire of all my worth,
of the shades of my mind, and the colors of my soul,
(red, yellow, black, white)
Draw me North!

O primal source of all that heals,
O person that redeems,
Take me East!

O Watcher of the deepest heart of mankind,
O Guardian of the Sacred Circle,
O Talking piece with Eagle feather,
O Initiator of the story's power,
O Telling of the legend of people and animals,
Fly me South!

Friend Contemplation

O true Friend,
O true revealer of my heart,
O true lattice for my soul's rose,
O joy of my time before heaven,
Braid!

O only prophet
of the logos and the rhema,
(speaker, carrier, listener)
Bind!

O tomb where beauty does not fade,
O epitaph where chiselled in its stone o'er the grave,
Loose!

O Suture of the surgeon's lancet,
O Critique of the artist's paint,
O Map of the compass spiritual quest,
O High places of new worship,
O Beginning from the end, circle us,
Tie!

Presence Contemplation

O true Presence,
O true healer,
O true voice,
O spirit of contemplation,
Rejoice!

O only builder
of the three mansions of the soul,
(heaven, earth, hell)
Restore!

O highest beauty of all created things,
O paradise of the seven heavens,
Repair!

O Subject of the child's dream,
O Object of the prophet's word,
O Deeps of onward wisdom,
O Healer of the Mother wound,
O Tryst with triune light,
Reunite!

River Contemplation

O true River,
O true waters flowing down,
O true legends of the deep,
O spirit of the mountain to the sea,
Sweep on!

O only four directions
of the four medicines,
(from innocence to strength)
It is the wind that moves the trees!

O waterhouse of all earth's unseen springs,
O portrait of the skies' bright indigo bead,
It is the earring of the Great Spirit!

O Visions of the tribal dance,
O Sweep of sunlight's fiery chance,
O Moon's sonata, rising true,
O Community that caused the wound,
O You shall heal it too,
Lamp to the darkness!

Section IV: Circle Keeping

My moon is blue tonight, its circle still:
I hold its breath within my circle's eyes,
cold glowing flame that stings into the frost . . .

—Emily Isaacson

Part One: Surreal Sage Smoke

Song Without Words

If I was a song
ruminating in the skies—
I would escape
before the wrath,
from every cage of darkness, binding.

Traipsing over the hills,
the larks are free,
without the prisons of humankind,
they are no prisoner
of the last rays of mango-shaped suns.

The sun is but an emperor of light,
he crowns the day, the earth, for all below:
the morning rising of the song birds
over the thunderous overture of night,
taking flight over oppression
and its henchmen,
leaving behind all that marked their sound
as a knarled word,
or a sum,
instead of a note. Sing to me softly, my note.

Singular Mendelssohn,
I wing free, whispering brown feathers,
singing of beings, a dream-catcher—
I hold a root that will grow
into a tree, a word-less song
to entwine me.

Sonnet of Tears

Along the Highway of Tears, far from home,
I was deep in my own heart as I hummed,
the cars in multicolored rhythm drummed
a stretch of road so lonely I could roam.
Yet, one car stopped and would not pass me by,
he motioned too, with ulterior name,
then signalled me, a moth unto his flame,
avoiding the dark rain, I sat inside.
As sea birds fly into the bulwark's brine
waters, cresting ocean, I was caught up
by the notion I was saved—and by love,
we struggled at the next stop 'neath the pines.
A silenced mind, I was no longer free,
beaten, my heart, was resting on his knees.

Part Two: Renaissance Remembrances

Even Water

I was walking from a desert oasis
where the leafy day occurs effulgently at will,
into the dry hot sand.
Men are thirsty—
with the kind of thirst that makes
you rant and rave with fever,
that even water cannot quench.

The prison chaplain had told me
that the men in prison cells
were desperate,
looking for any way
they could
to fill the burning desire
ravaging their flesh.

Desire,
you consume men
with the things they cannot have,
and then burn them
like a house to the ground.

Many Prisons

Groaning is the first language of desert—
of suffering beyond words.
Groaning is what must take me
beyond the self-pity and the despair
of the women's prison.
I begin to see visions,
maybe even hallucinations, heart-stopping.

There are many prisons;
but there is joy,
deepening and widening
the dimensions
in which I live and breathe.
The hurt and the pain will now seep
into the ground.

Desire,
I have not forgotten my mother,
no longer is my hair tangled
with my own sweat
and tears.

No More Tears

The children were separated
from their parents
whenever they were taken off
to juvenile hall.
They would not cry;
there are no more tears
where they now live.

The rooms are stark
as dormitories,
and there are bars on the windows.
There are places
no one can escape from,
and places everyone wishes
they could go.

Desire,
I thought my parents
would protect me from your grip,
but I too have wanted
more than is mine.

Traditions of a People

I receive the talking piece, aching
that what I see has not yet come to pass,
but it is coming.
All I have right now
is the practice of forgiveness—
forgive . . .
forgive . . .

I sing in the rolling purple night
of the traditions of a people
who have been told
there is no hope covering
and know only fear
in the ashes of a heart
that has grown cold.

Desire,
I walked away
from everything in life
that would subdue me.
I no longer need anything.

Lament

Call out in the night
as the watches begin
lift up your voices,
lift up your lament.
The prisoner's cry rings
as he is a human soul
with no recourse.

Held within the prison
of hatred and pain,
there is no way out
and no way in.
In my father's house I was trusted.
Now I meet the hard eyes
of suspicion and distrust.

Desire,
I conquered you long ago.
There is nothing I want now.
There is nothing you can offer me.
I will say no.

Destitute

Take me captive to you,
imprison me in darkness,
drag me from my home,
burn all I love,
until I am destitute.
Make my heart contrite,
batter my flesh, break me like glass.

The women of the prison
line up for breakfast.
Now regret is a toxic poison,
bitterness is a cup, difficult to drink—
resentment at hardship
is even worse;
but I am harder on myself than you.

Desire,
can you see me growing old
before your eyes;
did I know that those were cold lies
that I would gain everything.

The Homeless Camp

I am surrounded
by the patched summer tents
of a flapping tent city.
My cooking fire, it blazes
without going out,
orange flames
against the dark.

Burn in my belly,
medieval force
that propels me into the world
I don't understand;
turn me from apathy.
If there is a way to survive,
I will take it.

Desire,
I can't let my will
consume me or others,
so I yield to a deeper power
that calls my name at six a.m.

The Women's Shelter

They were yellowed in a drawer
when I found them,
there was something about the once
white eyelet curtains
that made me think of the past:
how a married woman once hung them
in the window.

They were like a shield over her eyes
from the sun, bearing good witness
that she had not forgotten the pledge.
But promises fade to presumption,
and now she was
rummaging in her purse for the
number to the women's shelter.

Desire,
there were large unwieldy doormats
to welcome the guests she expected,
the ones who never came,
the child she never had.

The Native Outcry

Abandoned by the ones who promised us
a future, we are once again alone.
We knew we could make a circle,
and that the medicine wheel
would heal us from despair,
that we could forge purpose
in the four directions.

The children take hands;
they believe we have a future
if we stand together,
but we have only the water
from our tower of streams and rivers,
the abiding plenty
of nature's storehouse.

Desire,
the promises you make
have grown shabby,
and we know you do not
love your victims.

The Indigenous Tree

There was a sacred day
when I found your tree—
I wish I did not have to dig up the roots
of colonization and then bury
them again. Now there are
many voices, sons of thunder,
wives of rain.

Will you walk healed, my children
of song? Grandchildren of chant,
the drumming keeps on—
will the Great Spirit answer?
He is like a gourd,
lighting our path
through the night.

Desire,
there is no over-consumption
of resources without
the corruption of those in power:
and we thought they were all that way.

Part Three: Native Land

The Loom of the North

Something is always
simmering on the black stove
and in the journal of time;
she wrote of
the shining northern purity
of a female icon—
love and sincerity
in the figurative,
stargazing in the field,
weeping at transgression:
the sorrow of her eyes,
the sweetness of her mouth—

Stretched on a loom,
the huge white cloth
of the North;
we were the threads,
short and long,
our ways
stretched across it.

Wilderness

In the dry hills,
lisped and forgotten;
sandy, and breathing
in rhythm,
a virgin forest
with biting cold
and feathery branches—
each night a gently
sloping gold:
the suitor of the sun
in full splendor,
the stars of
aspen night,
piercing the darkness
one by one,
and lullaby
soft-dreamed,
still—
downriver,
downwind,
a life of one's worth,
a thousand miles
into the wilderness
of soul.

House of the Snow

Canadian winter
flew down on the wings of an owl,
submerged a small settlement
in a blanket of snow:
riveted by icicles frozen
from the rooftops,
where fires blazed
in the hearth,
green and red holly
and cedar bracken
graced the mantelpiece.

The snowflakes,
silver
poignant and sure,
measured in time to
drifts of white
where footprints
were unique,
one by one
subdued
deep
and dreaming
in snow.

River Cabin

North as a place
in the mind
where a safe house
coexists
with a much-needed
wilderness.

Blackcap and
red huckleberry,
nettle and fern,
cascara, buttercup,
burnished hazelnut,
and red rose hips.

Peppergrass,
Indian plum
in an open wood,
dandelion suns dotting
the wild grass,
and coltsfoot,
inhabiting the shaded ground
of the river bank.

The trailing blackberry
wound its way
along the neck
of the forest;
its purple-seeded harvest
a steeped nectar
over the fire.

Portrait

At a high point,
I rode for three
miles, unhindered,
through the thrush altars
and golden grass,
the eucalyptus-hued
silhouette
like a small, undated
black and white
photograph:
over the Saskatchewan
fields of rye,
into the distance
on an old black mare.

New Moon

The watercolors
of the Arctic Inuit
bloom round
the cabin door,
a stream to cloak the
Northern star,
nursed in a pine cone.

And the moon was
round and full,
a silent song in a dusty sky
filled with regret and longing,
each night the close
to a gold-rimmed dream.

What we thought of Creator,
maker of the earth
and singer of the ancient song,
was a liturgy of legend
drummed in solemn chants.

We turned the pages of time,
and the fire burned,
the ground was
turned under
and the prayers
like seeds
beneath the earth
grew into a field,
row upon row:
became our sustenance.

Star of the Sea Art Gallery

Trembling aspens
rooted among the moss
and ferns,
the white-tailed deer,
elk and bear,
silent like the ethereal
white sun,
the boron of
Saskatoon bushes,
a Pleiades and Orion
to the solar
constellation
of immaculate
childhood:
sea stars left on an
old arctic bench.

Rockies

Stretched over the horizon
from a stone hunch,
a formidable cloak of gray
and insurmountable
face of time,
the mountains
congeal the rain into snow
and ice,
making the mortal
hemisphere feel
the pain of cold and
still,
swift
hunger.

Risen from the death
under a mantle of white,
the cliffs loom
precariously,
touching sun's
first light.

Bridle Of The North

In the reach of
St. Roch,
expect equilibrium:
two tunes,
strung
rhapsody—
true North,
true love—
under the twilight
of the
northern star.

The dance of
summer and winter,
the marriage of
spring and fall,
bringing forth
children
after a dream,
to equate
love and eternity.

O Immortal

Immortal God,
ever-present
crucifix:
be innocent of my blood;
omnipotent,
invisible,
the wind
round about us,
cloistering us,
inhabiting
the shores
of our nation,
indivisible.

Section V: A Handful of Sonnets

Over these flat, mud-crusted fields
in morning they fly . . .

—Emily Isaacson

Part One: Winsome Nostalgia

Remember me, though friendless now I be,
when through the parting sash I waved so cold,
and when the downpour drenched me growing old,
it was your friendship I desired to see.
Your chestnut hair was like the autumn's end,
then parted as a river from its source,
your red lips spoke in snows like holly boughs—
poisonous green, yet comely to defend.
My eyes have now been opened, I was fair
to every friend I valued in the mirror,
my foes live in a realistic fear
I'd intuit my neighbours and their cares.
If only I'd extend my hands in grace,
I'd look upon a multicultural face.

The light shone out a little bleary-eyed,
from every casement window to the night,
it was the little house that glimmered bright,
we walked the lake road to the water's side.
It was the home that we had waited for,
it spoke to us of hearth and firelight,
the attic rooms kept children within sight,
the plans we had would make us long for more.
Beneath the eaves the memories were dear,
and countless others had this way come by,
with dreams romantic, lovers that would tie
their hearts unto each other, ever near.
We counted every penny with intent,
but came up short, with modest discontent.

When I have lived my years, I shall recall
of days when I would not recant my youth,
the hours I walked among the sandy dunes,
observing gulls that flew 'till they were small
upon horizons far 'neath dusty moon.
My mother was the sea, my father, sun—
I was the morning light through seaweed dun,
that tides had strung the shore we walked so soon.
If anything in childhood I regret,
my life would be too sentimental now,
when auburn frames an alabaster brow,
the names of all my starfish I'd forget.
What word I spoke in child-like melody,
became the verse that echoed from the sea.

Ode to Canada

My country was the destination near—
of immigrant, traveller, visitors,
and men and women sojourned on our shore—
made haste from old dominions rung with tears—
They left in boats as Syrian refugees,
the dead of night had hid them, and they rowed,
arriving with their children in the flow
of time, through oceans, poverty's disease.
To freedom!—people called with libertine.
Their hearts were softened to a native land
where people stood together hand in hand.
Their eyes were opened, they began to sing—
We are the patriot wanderers home,
in all of us command our hearts aglow!

There was a light that burned upon the prow,
the figure of a woman in its mast,
in dark, the isle of drudgery was passed,
and ram-rod straight she stood with salted brow.
The moon reflected on her seeing eyes
that looked into the distance with constraint
the figurehead of politics restrained,
she was not fearful of their dreadful lies.
Unyielding at the storm of every task,
she sailed as ship 'Restorer' through each sea,
her silvered hair of wood hailed ocean's lea,
the water lilies bowed for living last,
forgotten, starboard's view of fading light:
today has gone, tomorrow will arise.

The city bourgeoned by the waterside,
an isle of apple blossom, steady pink,
and winter skated sorrow 'round the rink.
Through former age, in word and deed, now bide,
to resolution, cavalier and bold,
that evil will not fall upon the mild,
and vales of lilies grow 'till they are wild.
We picked fiery bouquets, as we were cold,
and mothers gathered families 'round the vase,
and walkers of the road were doubly blessed,
by nature's bounty, giv'n at their request,
a boy who heard the gilded ringing paused.
For history was reticent and kind
at island's song repeating on the mind.

When I would give my parting glance to thee,
when I would bid thee my austere good bye—
I give you my respect with lowered eyes—
passing by you, I would imagine me
with you, a better heaven than before.
I saw you rise to glory without qualm,
the storms of life had all resolved to calm.
Your aging rage had crashed upon the shore
as you conceded life was not to be
forever and forever of thy breath,
but families continue on into the next
years, and generations rise to thank thee.
When I would pay my last respects, in laud,
we all would give your well-deserved applause.

City of flowers, sweet moments at will,
remember me lonely as a kindness,
a sea-sick isle swept with reminiscence,
from starry wood-fenced meadow to the hill.
I played beneath the poplar trees at school,
a delicate child with gold braided hair:
I was your poet, knelt, composing there,
pupil of the largest transcendent pool.
Your children, Thetis and Saltspring, come by
for tea in a garden of fine incense,
steaming rose hips and lingering reasons
for conversing with a true butterfly:
sending you their translucent wing letters,
setting your thoughts free from iron fetters.

Lovely, my lovely when the night has passed,
I dream, though waking, my tears on your face,
I have lived my lifetime, and now your grace
has wakened me once more to autumn's last:
the leaves all turning as a crimson tide
vacating Dallas Point becomes the fall,
the moments before winter's silent call,
and the last mother stone cathedral's chide.
Her bells have rung out in the Sunday morn,
the whitened light through stained glass, glowing peers,
and falling snow will wait 'till late next year,
'till after the new dairy calves are born.
Fortuitous that I have heard you call,
before the ground is frozen, shadows tall.

Soldier-like, bravest man a rising moon—
backs to earth—there is a war—they'd open
their eyes, if on their eyes they could depend,
before all loyal sons lie in their tombs.
Hills, look to the hills—who'll join me, not one?
No longer have I a friend to think of,
all my patriot friends are fallen doves.
No one thinks better than of his own son,
a mother's tear would not forget this morn—
for here I stand, a lonely soldier last.
Fly from me enemy! Fly from my past!
I have courage for war until I'm torn,
and it is fully time, fly from me then.
Undeceive thyself from my contagion.

Part Two: Bergamot Brocade

The Freeman

Now to the world that has put me in chains,
I will laugh again, beyond this oak tree,
for I was once driven too, to be free—
there lies another prison with trowel:
there lies another logic that compels,
when forced to plant a marigold, plant ten,
throw seeds into the ground beyond land's bend;
my father, in the harvest time it tells
you were on a ladder of broken rungs,
chores burden you when you are ancient now,
with all the winds that have passed through your boughs.
You helped right the fallen trees, roped their trunks
so now they're back to back in allegiance;
no longer fallen, in a freedom stance.

A voice cries out, I dare not turn my head,
the abyss is deep and to its depths I see
it red with flame or blood! Turn away thee,
fatal path, woe to those who want me dead.
I shall not touch the wound that gored so deep:
not faithful love—the duty of a wife,
she's fortunate without their passion's strife.
Incumbents of religion now would weep,
if no one would oppose mental cruelty;
for this has been a battered, silent church,
not one voice uttered not one febrile word,
to encourage some brutal brass fealty.
There is always tomorrow to resolve
the hearts of our dear marriages dissolved.

The horses, stirred up, in the darkening France,
went thundering down the hill every which way,
I hid in terror from their highland neigh,
behind a trunk, while holding to a branch.
It was magnolias upon the tree,
their fragrance was as gospel to my heart,
rivalling holy scriptures from the start,
the gardener had planted much for me.
Without regret, I knew that I was saved
from illiterate end without a book—
for I was cloaked in words, ink shod my foot,
without debt, in the black, I calmly stayed.
For writing is divine when free from fear;
reflection's more successful in the mirror.

If ever you were mine, don't leave me pearls,
my eyes brim with tears at your advancing
years, your leopard prints and tango dancing
into the looking glass with whitening curls.
You once were very beautiful and sweet,
the men that took your picture held their heads,
they courted with intentions you were wed,
they benefitted you with Purdy's treats—
How momentary is a compliment
unless a woman's character is built,
a castle on the sand is anchored silt—
foundation of a home is wet cement.
Oh now, my darling, do not look at me,
for I am beautiful, but never seen.

When I started at this one quarter note,
perfect order of a five finger scale,
it became something of a killer whale
by Beethoven, black and white emotive
played for background noise called the Für Elise.
My classical training at dawn each day
never let me forget my practice way—
my gilded lily was a fleur-de-lis.
For I was only small and a witness—
you are my father and you put my first
coat on my back before we went to church,
my brief spoken prayers were the crucifix—
beyond religion to the spirituals—
lend me your depth, I practice rituals.

If you have loved me, I have not complied,
although I dance with you to our first tune,
float by on the canals beneath the moon,
the oar for this gondola you supplied.
The yellow coat I thoughtfully recall,
I hung my reverie on your door hook,
I remembered hungrily every book
you recommend, every word read, the small
bowed tell-tale things of yours I don't forget:
your leather briefcase, your love of dark
coffee, Turkish tea that started it all—
the contest of wills to see who was met
by strangers in foreign lands and who stayed
home. But we both had degrees of straying.

A Handful of Blackberries

The last of light has faded with the night,
and shadows disappear into the dark,
the sun is now forgotten like last lark,
and rounded moon is captive to this light.
Walking with a handful of blackberries,
I'm nestled deep inside my guarded stance,
I'm made of stone, unblinking in a trance,
I wrestled with the thorn bush then tarried.
My artisan bread contains the berries
and the last cream rose petals from the arch
over the garden's entrance in the park
there, where my truest friend was once married.
We walked on friendship's path of watermere,
and contemplated future moments dear.

I am an agent blind of all sadness,
I am deaf of mournful mysteries! Still
of misery made from a cup of chilled
white wine—one dime, recalled work in darkness.
Soul, I cannot tell. I am urged to run
by impetuous breath and false decree;
I fall and fall in swift descent to thee.
I am at the bottom of a well, done,
better if I pull myself up by my
bootstraps and go down to the potter's brown
stone house. If sometimes, I dare turn and frown,
it is that I have never met the sky:
pots and works of clay that were amber red.
Potter with so much coloured glaze, my head!

The clock chimes eight, and through the window pane,
the light so dim, my dear, at evening's end,
and purposefully twilight bows its head;
it never poured anointing on the lane,
but walking to this antique house you came,
with walking stick beside you striking stone,
and rivulets of water ran alone,
across the cobbled pathway just the same.
You saw me through an uncorrupted lens,
I was an age-old book you'd read before,
from the glass teapot, wintermint was poured,
we spoke in lowered tones at time's expense,
before the cherished crystal breaks and cries,
a boreal reflection of the skies.

Your last word in this pallid hospice realm
was miniscule as round millet is small,
impossible to catch beyond the hall,
yet indicative of golden ship's helm,
voyage looming onward into heaven,
far beyond this one sombre meaning filled
room, fragrant with flowers on the white sill,
from each child beneath your heart, all seven.
In righteous clothing you are finely dressed,
there was a call to you once with meaning,
past the world's inebriated dreaming;
what word of praise to give the very blessed?
The last moment with you I saw a door
you opened to the sick, the homeless, poor.

Part Three: Classic Shades

Go catch a mouse in your medieval life,
for Persian cats these days have not changed tin
to bronze; I would that you go out, yet in
you come, no alchemist of human strife.
You chased a dandelion's last feather,
and watched the drooping rose lay down its head,
you curled up in a cozy basket bed,
your down was damp from terrible weather.
What'ere I wish, it likely will not be,
and I could cross my fingers, hope to spy,
while serving chlorophyll in salmon pie,
around a cat as difficult as me.
With luck, she never actually offends,
she utters loud meows with no pretense.

Many red apples of your orchard grow,
each rust variety I could desire,
eaten fresh or roasted over the fire,
glow in deep burgundy, magenta, rose.
You harvest the supernatural book,
to feed a town not far from the river,
from the King James' version, reading scripture—
an Abbott was once fjording the clear brook.
They sold your ripe fruit at the marketplace,
McIntosh, Spartans, piled high in wood bins—
you were a ruffian who's forgiven,
you offered help to the lady with lace,
she crocheted doilies for your table,
where the fruit bowl would sit and be stable.

If I am set in my maturing ways,
I may be now an octave not a note,
lest drawing years now catch me by the throat,
and victimless the world would seldom stay,
held dear, a crime of passionless embrace.
The echoes of the weapon on my neck,
the tumbling fingers keeping me in check,
the slant upon my skin of scar's necklace.
I would be still a frightened Northern star,
now gleaming through each variegated tree,
aurora borealis glowed briefly
if I was to imagine life unmarred.
You sent me sterling, my lover was new,
I was to sail in a cedar canoe.

When you retreat alone into the wood,
you are familiar with places forlorn,
you bow your silver horn, a unicorn,
and the poetic verse is now your food.
Look into the bright spiritual domain,
and see if heaven's walls are high and close,
see if the door is open thee or closed,
look to the tower, the castle maintained
an archer, with a rainbow, sky to sky,
seek in thine arsenal the armour shined
for all of sixty years—thou art still mine,
beneath all sorrows that the poor would spy,
for we are never cruel nor cold, betrothed,
our hearts glow with our kindness and our love.

Beside the red warmth of your roaring hearth,
I draw myself up to your friends' circle
and the firelight dims to blue and purple,
the flickering stories revealed your mirth.
On the avenue of constellations
I walk upon the stars on the pavement,
everyone has a name in the cement,
their gold street of stellar revelations.
There is a home in your soul of contrasts:
I find a virtue in your caverns dark
that shines, a vein of gold within a lark,
some streak of light made you lonely grasses,
where the wild birds would swoop and make their nests
here the poorest peasants make their homes best.

When you are near to the tiny new babe,
extravagant love in coming to earth,
the incarnation of his virgin birth,
the light of the gospel that will not fade . . .
Listen to the reason for his kindness
to us: the season of rejoicing tells
of gifts from the Magi, frankincense smells
of beauty, myrrh restores our innocence.
Gold is the enduring royalty now,
an immediacy with God's future—
our lives are now restored to us, sutured,
and sin is no longer the altar bowed.
To the underworld, death! For Christ is born—
if he should then die with bright crown of thorns.

There are black figs that grow from thistle's brier,
pears ripen from ev'ry Calvary's thorn,
there is a land called heav'n—it is the morn—
and it descends on us within our mire.
My pristine view could spy its pearlesque gate,
from place of inky darkness I would look
from page to page inside an aging book,
the twelve tall oaken wall clocks growing late.
We don't aspire as children to be short,
nor looked upon with unrealistic eyes,
nor told our Saviour bleeds for us and cries,
not when the adults do console with port.
I thought I'd leave some burgundy for you,
or seltzer water with a lime ice cube.

Now to my end I come in stately black,
for I am but a prisoner of this earth,
I can't escape its clutches or its wrath,
nor any of its loves, nor laughs, nor births.
I bear the lovely France a final fleur,
I witness of this hour before the flame,
for all my visions have been of one cœur—
I cry to God, unyielding of his name.
Do not my hands untie, lest I recant—
for I am but a bird that cannot fly.
Do not relent, for I shall not repent;
my sweetest fame is written now on high.
You look upon my pure and martyred face,
that in the flame of love has found its grace.

If I have loved you in a thousand ways,
I have lit a thousand candles for you.
I have made a fire and cooked a beef stew.
My heart is sincere, my mind never strays:
I would but give a thousand gifts that morn,
if my life held you in one thousand wings,
if I gave away a half-dozen things,
my sentimental songs you would not scorn.
One thousand carollers stood at your door,
there was no unserved guest, no unmet need
before your home of hospitality,
and each one ringing louder than before.
I'll laugh again before my life is through,
because you have loved me and I've loved you.

O flame that circles me—O wisdom's light,
seeking the way through my utter darkness,
hurtling from the outside through the starkness
to the inside of my heart, a dark night
of the soul cannot distance purer thee—
for I would write in ink your mind untold,
and fashion you as from clay to the world,
until the blind could endless, boundless see.
Through obsession I would find my novice;
she would be of one love and one desire,
lone in a convent cell she would retire.
She is blessed olive without one vice,
of a still-chaste, and contemplative place—
now humans could not boast to see this face.

Section VI: Dancing in the Dark

bathe
these dark-eyed angels
in the dust . . .

—Emily Isaacson

Part One: Rustic Maize

Dimes

Multicoloured Maize

I can work for dimes,
I am as swift as a centaur
with a bow; I can read the skies—
I know when it will rain or snow.

Blue Maize

I will ride through the streets
before dawn,
and drop newspapers before people awake,
at their oblique doors.

Maple Tree Angel

I lift the curse over you
of blistered feet and bruised shins,
of the tiredness that makes women fall
down in a dead faint.

Newsprint

Multicoloured Maize

Whatever you print,
I will run with it,
declaring the facts are before you
to all newsprint readers.

Blue Maize

It will be a decade
before I tire of being first;
a messenger before the morning's
commencement.

Maple Tree Angel

I lift the curse over you
of being driven by fear,
that whatever is asked of you
you must comply without question.

Small and Shy

Multicoloured Maize

Who created the sky?
It is small and shy
at first light,
then later brilliant.

Blue Maize

There is no breathing space
without you;
you are the breath I breathe
mile upon mile.

Maple Tree Angel

I lift the curse over you
of a life like an athlete,
who pushes their body and their pain
to the limit of their endurance.

Rugged

Multicoloured Maize

The rain and the snow
cannot stop my engine
from running continually
all night, rugged over the rock salt.

Blue Maize

I am in and out of shadows,
feeling the rough bark of tree branches
with the moon my only companion.
I will not forget your love.

Maple Tree Angel

I lift the curse over you
of a life in the dark,
of blinds drawn,
and the fear of light.

One Minute Per House

Multicoloured Maize

I drive myself on, through the night,
with only one minute per house,
remembering that to be meaningful
I need only breathe pure prayer.

Blue Maize

The media is driven,
and relentlessly new each day,
but the stories are gritty
and full of the harshness of real life.

Maple Tree Angel

I lift the curse over you
of the unrelenting menial nature
of hard work,
and of a heavy yoke.

Early Light

Multicoloured Maize

Walk with me a few paces;
see how the mountains reveal their glory.
The early light drenched them, over
my numb fingers and hypothermic toes.

Blue Maize

A young man calls after me,
his name is Michelangelo.
He painted the sky by hand,
and sculpted each cloud; remember his name.

Maple Tree Angel

I lift the curse over you
of feeling like your goals as an artist
are just out of reach,
somewhere with the paint and brushes.

Wages

Multicoloured Maize

Break up the ground for the gourds
corn, and beans beneath the evergreen;
we will eat the Three Sisters, come fall
like chiefs at the harvest.

Blue Maize

If I wished to buy a loaf of bread
from my wages of twenty cents a house,
I would have to go to twenty-five houses.
I might think, why bother to eat bread?

Maple Tree Angel

I lift the curse over you
of the high cost of living,
of having to skip meals and go hungry
to make ends meet.

Mundane

Multicoloured Maize

My fear of the mundane
has made me travel at the speed of light,
in the twinkling of an eye, with nerves of steel,
undaunted by normal folk.

Blue Maize

I am saving desperate women
on street corners,
alerting endangered victims to foul play,
playing a threatening dame in back alleys.

Maple Tree Angel

I lift the curse over you
that you will go under for giving
a kind word to the homeless still straggling
in the street with their blankets, come morning.

Misfit

Multicoloured Maize

I am part of a new group
of nameless, faceless people,
a usually invisible family of misfits,
a cog in the machine.

Blue Maize

I don't ever quit, even in the hot sun,
even if it pours sheets of rain in the autumn,
even if I fall in the winter;
I am your witness, with a bird's eye view.

Maple Tree Angel

I lift the curse over you
from rising in the dead of night
to carry out a long arduous task
that on some days seems occult.

News Copy

Multicoloured Maize

I wake up in the dark,
and hit the floor running;
I will carry out today
all God's asking me to do.

Blue Maize

I will be the first
to receive the news copy,
I will be the first to hear
and then run with it for hours.

Maple Tree Angel

I lift the curse over you
from travelling into the land of the dead.
The one provision given to us
was enough for the journey.

Olive Oil

Multicoloured Maize

I light my lamp,
I remember to pray:
the olive oil will never run out,
the cistern will not run dry.

Blue Maize

The symbol of my commitment
to purity are the white garments
that have never been worn,
the cream cloths that have never been torn.

Maple Tree Angel

I lift the curse over you
of seven years of slavery
that represents our slavery to sin.
There was a coin in their mouths.

Section VII: Great Lakes Prayer

strains from
the gestation of night,
where auroras
melt the sky . . .

—Emily Isaacson

Part One: Artisan Immersive

Listener

I am Listener.
I am living on the shore of Lake Superior.
Here, in my garden,
all I profess is to hear.

I hear the voices of deity,
the voices of people,
the complaints of citizens,
the travellers on.

I will be here
until hope rises.
When you speak,
I will listen.

All I profess as my payment is love,
and I have the key
to the gate of love:
mine is a steady gaze to the Prophet.

Translate

I am Listener,
living out my life
through both blessing
and hardship on the lake shore.

It is simple to think
that it is easier
not to hear the voices,
not to understand their meanings.

I will wait
for the understanding
to translate emotion and thought
into riddles that bait the heart.

What was once worth nothing at all
is now of great value.
I have mentioned this
to the Prophet.

Pelagic Prayers

I have cried for you,
you see my tears that fill great lakes
to the prehistoric brim,
and the concentric circles repeat.

At the thunder of one stone
these pelagic prayers
are a wanting to be free from earth,
as a listener of the waters.

I listen, as the wind
in the trees on Lake Superior
ruffles my bald head and eagle feathers
and dares me to soar.

I will ask the Prophet
to enter through the gate of love:
I have the gold key that opens
the silver gate.

Fresh Water Tears

I wring out my sorrow
like fresh water tears into the lake
from the mines of my heart.
My notions of catharsis are repetitive.

As the seasons change,
my hair fades to grey;
I sit by the draped window
of my lake house.

I am Listener,
and those who notice I care
are my friends,
they receive the outpouring.

I will implore the Prophet
to pour out
the wine of the presence,
that we might be filled anew.

The Passion of the Jews

I listen to the echo of the Prophet.
Her voice was once a powerful
kindness to the passion of the Jews.
She understood their success and their failure.

I speak out my joy received
and my praise;
when others listen,
I commend them.

Thus my solemn certainty
of the past and the future:
doves were sacrificed on the altar
for my child once—

Birds, swimming across the blue—
that the righteousness
of my son
could not be traded for jewels.

Analgesic Soprano

I listen to the sounds of the lake.
Her voice is like camphor,
an analgesic soprano
that sounds its cool note.

My chronic pain
disappears with the numbing
of society's ailment—
the pain of its divorce from God.

Thus my note to the Prophet,
that there was an impassable divide
between humanity and the divine,
and a dove was sacrificed on the altar—

There was a perfect health and purity—
that a dove's righteousness
took the place of my son
so he would not have to pay later.

Accomplish Something

I will listen each day
because you are
full of new material,
a maker of art.

You want to accomplish something
in me that I could not do on my own.
You know me quite well,
from the very beginning.

Thus I asked to be your servant,
I refused to leave
when you offered me my freedom;
I am your bond-servant.

I follow you around,
and follow your example.
When you go swimming,
I swim too, like a duck in the same pool.

Buried Secrets

I am Listener.
I have a secret buried deep
like a seed in this old house,
on the shore of one of the Great Lakes.

A vintage wedding diamond is in my safe,
one that belonged to my mother,
and was given to my wife
before she died of cancer.

The stone sits alongside a few First Editions,
a manuscript I wrote,
and all my contemplative notes
from the Prophet.

Our painting in words
may outlive the painting collection that ages,
my wife's photographs that fade,
but only if they die and come to life—as a seed.

Cedar Chest

Now I bow my head,
for I have grown old
on the shore of Lake Superior,
and my secrets will outlive me.

In the cedar chest in our bedroom
are still my wife's finely folded
winter clothing, and the rugged scent
of cedar oil and the lake.

All I have kept of her is in this chest,
her elegant handwriting, her journals,
the book of black and white
photographs of her childhood.

She wanted me to remember her young
and beautiful, steady and graceful;
not the moments of pain,
but a butterfly with wings.

What Fear Will Do

There is a whisper from the past,
that we must overcome an old curse.
That is why I pray
and invoke the blood of Christ.

Was it the prayer
that death would not overpower us
that lead me to pray for my wife
when she was dying?

It is what fear
will do to a man;
what I was willing to ask of God
when she was ill.

I will never understand why he let her die,
why when I prayed, he did not heal her.
I stayed with her body for two days
before I let her go.

Section VIII: A Mosaic of Words

Under the northern lights,
the colour dances,
strains from
the gestation of night . . .

—Emily Isaacson

Part One: Earthen Library

Call to the Poets (Fantasia)

Where are the poets?
Where are their deep sonorous voices,
their caves hidden far within mountains?

Poets, I call you.

Where do they cry so no one hears,
espousing the distance
between God and humanity?

Poets I call you by darkness,
I call you by light.

Their burning embers are the eyes
that can see,
unblinded by night.

Poets, I call you by
your multi-faceted names,
your dominions,
your many lives in former places.

You and your spoken word
work their way into
the sands of our minds
as the sea—our castles

demolished each day
and washed away
into Solomon's tomb,
where his wives glow with aqua stones.

If a poet would speak,
the poem would live
in our shallow heartbeats, in the deep
trenches of our borders.

May I Ask? (Cavatina)

If you're no good
for advice,
I'll answer myself—
you put the lettuce
in the freezer
(in a moment of senility).

They say the diet started
when margarine
was invented.

You say women
are quite
seductive to you—
but only as muses.

They stand straight
and silent, unmoving,
as mannequins
in the supermarket.

Caveat Emptor (Arioso)

I was a woman
of no ambition,
few dreams,
and even fewer dollars.
Let me check my gage and
see if I could even drive
to the next gas station.

It was a fault
that could never stick
to my collar or my uniform
(but this is not a fashion show),
speaking in signs

to the see-through
iridescent ones,
downloading elegant
robes online,
runes delineating
my spiritual rights
instead of rumours—

oils dripping, salmon flipping,
and ancient medicine
echoing the osteoblasts
of my bone.

Sinew to sinew,
we were glossy horses
among the six hundred
that belonged to a prince.

A Hearthstone (Largamente)

Earl Gray tea has an em dash
with two doses
of bergamot—
sidling with the milk of almonds
in my mug.

It is a hearthstone,
this weight in my chest—
I'll not mention
it to anyone
if I am your architect.

Heaven has a good
house plan,
and a pierced heart,
bleeding on a tree.

If you died
with your head on my shoulder
I'll not mention
it to anyone.

I will sing louder
and louder
until I drown you
in bergamot.

A Heart of Swans (Pensato)

When I saw two swans
in loving embrace,
I realized where
the heart shape came from.

The distance of my heart
from yours
is no further than
a swan's neck.

A swan has no more salty beauty
than is mirrored
in the waters below
or the sky above.

Water and sky
are both icy blue
as the cold
when I don't love you.

New or Old? (Misterioso)

You woke up
very early in the morning
for *The Gorgeous Nothings*.

There was a *Girl Reading*
in an entire library
of aunts reading
small girls.

You didn't want
me to read her
when she was so young.

Perhaps she was
uncomposed
like a scrap of an envelope.

She was unselfconscious
at that age;
they all are,
and are cream paper.

She is a lithe sunrise
springing over the roof,
diminutive unless
she wears orange.

When she was
old enough
I slipped her
a scrap of an old
envelope.

She wrote something
on it—
something that made
subtlety exist
every day of the week.

I read her Mother Goose
until she owned it
and could repeat it on any day
that was gray.

Her grandmother
took the envelope
and held it over the stove
until it burned—
a bright flash
turned to ash.

Monarch in the Subway (Da capo aria)

If I was reading,
I could be pouring over
any number of the two million
items put out that day:
as factual news article,
a joke, a myth,
a flinty poem,
a journal by someone
more innocent than I,
a novel about partners
I don't have.

If I was dancing,
nothing would sway me
(like a sway back)
deterring me from the barre,
closing my eyes
to the ballet in leotard.

If I had a camera,
in black and white, my dextrous fingers
would uncoil, strand by strand—
and, a passenger
in the subway,
I would lift my eyes
to notice a monarch butterfly
with cloudy wings,
parched,
dying on the sidewalk.

How can I capture you;
I can only
offend you with a lens,
and phone the metropolitan
to offer them your beauty's sleep.

I Heard the Owl Call My Name (Pasticcio)

The owl that you hear
two-hoots
so loud,
calling me,
that it echoes through
the whole town
of Stratford-upon–Avon—he flies
when all are asleep.

While he flies,
no one ever gets sick,
no one is tired
or sorry they were born,
has a face in a frown,
or walks upstairs and down,
all alone and forlorn,
when all are asleep.

The owl flies outside society,
his breath you will not see;
he is hidden deep
inside the bracken inside me,
saving his charges from leers,
brushing the grasses as spears,
eloping with the night wind's sound
when all are asleep.

A Patient Moment (Cabaletta)

I, the invalid,
am in good company
with a maze of sparkling hallways,
a hundred sterile hospitals,
beady-eyed doctors
with good bedside manners,
a host of diseases
to occupy my chart,
and nurses in a platoon,
their dozen thermometers
with or without mercury.

Do I want a life
with or without charity?
With or without
the poison,
dripping from the ceiling?
Formal or casual?
With or without
the trouble?
Ironed or wrinkled?
or somewhere in between.

Still Learning You (Verismo)

There is a curtain between us;
it has been there for ages,
and I have a priest
with a rope around his foot.
Unless he dies, he'll
be here with a word for you.

There is a calm upon
the stage with purposed eyes,
the locked jaw backdrop,
the bright lights, the wooden skull.
Unless the director dies, he'll
be here with an impression of you.

A cinder lights
the rough incense, thin, papery
and smoke twilled.
The sandalwood is all
you have in the ink-black—
you wear a mask; you keep insisting
you have beautiful dreams
as they smoke,

when they are quite terrible.
You awake and wish
you had never lived,
unless I can recall you
quite young in your oyster, before
your defence mechanism
crystalized calcium, layer upon layer,
prophesied like nacre,
formed a pearl.

Acknowledgement (Ossia)

I don't cry here
anymore,
the tears have turned
to salt on an old woman's
parchment face,
she became a pillar
of beeswax,
she has an unclaimed wit,
her wick has never been burned,
her lilies in the garden grow wild.

Nobody said,
"I do," and ate the potatoes with gravy,
no one stretched out their hand
with a band
of limitless gold.
(Binding the unexpected.)

She is an archangel now,
fluttering about the house—
her white hair flecked
and distressed
as a vintage memoir.

Part Two: Fading Town

The Shoe Tree

They say the heroin addicts
in this town
tied all these shoes together
by hand,
and threw them into the
branches of a tree.

There must have been
a hundred pairs
in a large elm
full of shoes,
each one speaking of someone
without shoes.

Your name was Friday.
You were sitting in the
doorway when I found you,
you had walked a long way,
and your shoes were
dusty and torn,
the tongues gaping wide
over your bare feet.

There was a thought
that someone should buy
you another pair,
and should that
someone be me?

You were a lost boy,
and I was a shoe tree,
waving my arms,
insisting there are lots of shoes
for everyone.

Dragons in the Swamp

I thought skunk cabbage
was as white inside
as a sepulchre,
with a stench of the dead,
and rigid, upright
with nowhere to lay its lead.

The dragon of the swampy
black mud depths
is not depravity kind—
yet shall sin unwind
in her arsenic boots.
She had a cadmium modem,
so she told me,
that made her connected
to every other living thing.

They all dashed and bashed
her head,
until it was bent
and yellow—still breathing,
but putrescent,
still living, but unwilling,
unyielding.

Dragons in the Caves

There was a long tunnel
of connected caves,
where dragons lived by the sea.
Their mica ores flamed like nostrils.

I found the morning
where the smoke was rising
from their sulphurous mouths;
I found the evening,
the color of copper moths,
and sinewy green flesh—

What unknown light is walking
down the road?
It must be only a stranger's light;
if it had relative form or
were in any way known to them,
they would swallow
the poor person whole,
unless he was hiding
in a hole somewhere.

Before the Fire

There was a vandalised wall
between my heart
and my mind.
The graffiti colored wall drove
believers underground
for fear of persecution.

Few continued on in this vein
of silence over spiritual matters,
of quiet church,
humming the great hymns of the faith
in reservation
behind bolted doors.

When the wall came down,
missionaries came
like tiny people,
only for us to tell them
there was no watermelon
on this side of the wall before now.

They talked about Creation,
but we had only heard
of evolution.
Their script
was to smile, accept us,
and invite us in.

We were an acceptable darkness,
with poverty of religion,
no candle to see by,
like being married
with no wedding rings
and no church.

Then there was a bonfire,
and people surrounded it
with their hands stretched out;
better to be warm, we thought,
than cold.
Now we could sing louder.

Alleluiah, alleluiah
rang over the hills
of Germany:
it was a sad and glorious song.

The Cupboard

The doors of my cupboard
are an insect's wings,
small, illusive,
and things of flight—
catching light and darkness, swinging
open so everyone can see
what I keep hidden—
the neat Ikea bowls and plates
in orange and blue.

I thought they were relatively ordinary,
as a dragonfly over a lake,
nothing to mention,
but others, with nostalgia, finger them,
running their fingers over porcelain,
and put the bowls on their heads
like Jewish prayer caps—
then parade around,
boasting of plates in bright colours.

Frosted with emotion,
there is nothing in my mind.
It has all been emptied
and pilfered bare by scavengers
who saw a hole in the cupboard door
and helped themselves.

They even tried to put
their own things in my cupboard,
while I practiced meditation
as a skilful cover-up.

Now they fly like insects
on insect's wings—
tiny, whining, and growing smaller
in the distance.

Dancing in the Dark

I woke up while it was still dark
each morning, to have a quiet time
in the silent space in my mind,
before the window
closed to my towheaded child.

The child in me is naive,
wears her mother's clip-on earrings,
carries God under her arm
like a ragged teddy bear,
lives among communists,
and they make her spiritual life
as illegal as eating communion bread.

She might dance
when no one is around,
in a spinning skirt,
a Jewish circle dance in glory,
a cherubic gold-tinged angel.

Her name is Israel—
she might sing to her
audience of one,
as if her heart was new jade,
and a gift.

He was writing in the dust.
"What did I write?" he asked.
"Chalcedony," she answered,
tracing his face,
"the blood stone."

Her favorite book
was not supposed to be the Bible,
so she was hiding
paperbacks under the bed,
and they were dog-eared.

There was a day
when she would sing,
in unfaltering alto
at church—
it marked her as a composer.

No more rejection hummed
the radio, when she was twenty-five
and her latest song was a hit.
She was no longer a recluse,
but can anyone see her dancing in the dark?

If I Was Frost

Dedicated to Anna Frost

I knew it was almost winter
when the ground I walked on
was starched and stunted with ambiguity.

There was a mist over the trees,
like an iron's steam,
or a halo's sheen,
or a vision of a train appearing
and blurring the scene.

If I was my great-great-grandmother
she would not be less reticent,
less dulcet, or less articulate
than I in green—
the color of an undersea garden.

She sits at the kitchen table
and can crochet—
there is always much to do,
but she finds the time.
No one ever compliments
her work, but no one paid her either.

If I was Anna Frost,
my heart would linger
behind me in the field of snow,
because she is too shy to see
the future.

My mind would move
from room to room,
because it is like dancing.

My arms would rise up
to explain a mutual story
about one of our own.

My legs would fly out
in sinewy regality
like I was a flapper dancing the
Charleston,
when really I had died.

I would lay flat,
and covered with frost
as a winter's landscape,
frozen hair,
dressed in my wedding gown,
missional ivory.

The Fading Town

You'll get used to me,
mile upon mile,
you'll get used to my crown,
glittering beneath the ground.

I died a long time ago,
an elderly persecuted ego,
with a city built up within me,
and a fading town on the outside.

The trampled outskirts
were far into the marshlands,
and the herons waved their weeping wings,
and swallows croaked—
the frogs would sing.
The victuals of seed
and steel-red berry, beyond
the unutterable wounding
of latent hunger.

You'll get used to the mighty Stave,
thundering into the open hands
of the powerless,
of the long winding roads
in the damp country,
and the agricultural bushel.

The horses sniff the wind—
they are travellers too,
galloping into the lower field
at night, like we are powerful,
of intellectual orbits
like the long line
of poplars striking the sky.

Off Stage Right

The year had trickled by like a blue cord,
Jasmine's dark hair having grown
another four inches,
thick and shiny,
it was bound up in a bun with ribbons
and bobby pins every afternoon.

In the cold day, the ballet
seeped like liquid violet
across the nutcracker floor:
slowly, the studio—
one mirror after another—
caught the fading reflection . . .
one, two, three, pirouette—
in miniscule the refraction
plays an aging suite—
the classroom an echo,
in black and white—the note
a second tilt to toe bent—
one right arm after another,
one ribbon black, the other pink—
in the light, one carbon copy per minuet—
alone and still, the movement
just a tiny gold adept step
into the soul of arabesque.

I would die for the Mona Lisa,
Jasmine thought—and only
the ignorant don't know
that art is worth more than one body,
and blissfully they turn away.

Weep Salt

I am a foreigner in my own country—
my starch gives me
a pleasant consistency,
and I am stirred again and again
over the portable stove.

There are oats in my bones,
my character insists.
Some women weep salt
while they cook;
they could scarcely
hope for dark bread
and now make fibrous porridge.

The liquefied starch
is sweet as water,
and our minds
were hoping they would be
unaffected by its absence.

I am a foreigner in my own country—
without my rough bowl of gruel.

Section IX: Postmodern Poems

be rich and warm in the
firelight and evergreen:
crimson, emerald, and gold,
radiant in the arabesque of time . . .

—Emily Isaacson

Part One: Canadian Eclectic

Grey Jay

Dedicated to Robert Bateman

Whispering trees, there was someone lost:
how did I help him when he had so far to walk
to return to civilization, so long the road?
I flew from branch to branch
and curiously gripped the moss.
There was nothing I could say, I do not talk,
my intelligence has never been measured by my foes
or by my friends: my tiny boreal heart would dance

at last measure, if you need me near
I will fly to you, on waiting wing
and soar from rise to rise,
I would redeem your final crumb.
There is a friend in my bird body, dear
who would endeavor to save your life and bring
you all the way from sunset to sunrise—
while the moon was an even reflection of the sun.

When you have travelled far as the sea foam,
or into the wilderness where time and doubt linger,
and death draws near your humble dwelling:
a jay's brightness is stark—Away from us, O death!
the dark has no figment that finds in us a home.
The young lad reaches out his finger,
and the Whiskey Jack is from the sky felling,
my song belays my quiet and sonorous breadth.

Common Loon

It was haunting: a voice of the North had a face—
sounded its melancholy across the lake,
echoes of the fringe of black and white plumage in its wake,
the light and dark unmasked in queenly pace.

It was now summer and the campers had returned.
As the nature seekers pitched their tents from off their backs,
in the wilderness of the Adirondacks,
on Lake George, it was the iconic figure in black:
a miracle of crescendo in the sky concerned.

They had expected her classic portrait through the wine,
the deep oil on canvas, the triune colour,
her hidden nest near the forested body of water,
reflecting the wild and winsome throughout time.

Mournful, her loyalty resonated.
She carried her young under her wings,
she glided in a serene wake of water rings;
she was after the profundity of life without things,
and the North contracted, procreated.

Snowy Owl

Majestic was the span of the snowy owl's wing—
a vast country stood strong and true,
its strength throughout the Arctic ranges was omnipotent,
hunter of the wild hare, the fox spent,
it has no predator, nor silent does it sing.

Winter had a velvet glove on an iron hand—
the large owl in white grew pale with time,
hovering above the lamplight's glow sublime,
the second owl had markings of the mysterious wild
with golden eyes reveling in the harsh and mild,
rising into raptor heights above the land.

A predator that does not mind the ice,
the owl's feet are feathered,
it observes its wisdom weathered,
it has precision in a grip of vise.

What government could mind me in its double-bind:
the wisdom beating one last snowy breath,
the essence of fidelity's deafness,
unrelenting winter was never kind,
the field of night beneath the moon unwinds.

Canada Geese

All fly, and toward the North, for it is spring,
above our wings, there is a sun-filled sphere,
where the night echoes the moon,
the fire echoes the wind,
the ocean echoes the rain,
the snow echoes the mountain—
we travel boundless, here;
our cries, now unrelentless, ring.

All fly, then northward, steady on,
it is our v shaped form that maps the skies
with steady beating of our now harbinger eyes,
will you join with us, one and all—
as the sun will fill the bright noon's pall.

As the light fills the meadows of Canada with down,
each martyred watershed from Vancouver Island
to the Yukon, spirited hears
our honking masses, landing cries
of freedom on the muddy iridescent banks.

We do not cower, break our ranks with fault,
but we have taken to the heavens' sweeping finish,
and the lacquer of earth's rusty varnish,
with courage from of old—
let our biology turn bold
as light with salt:
in our handsome breast, untarnished,
and beneath our webbed feet
the country grows warm, and warmer still,
and the goslings follow sweetly.

Black-capped Chickadee

In the bitterest winter, there is a black-capped song:
chickadee-dee-dee calls the small bird,
there is no place in Canada it cannot be heard;
a two-tone melodic, she is constant at the bird feeder,
prized in her bravado toward other birds, she is a stalwart leader.
Unselfconscious now, sing along!

Her mighty heart flies on wing to a waiting child,
her impeccable spring attire is gray with a black crown.
Both the urban store, or the rural cache feed her,
to a tent, cottage, or castle she is a dependable regular.
This rock-star is dressed up for every occasion on the town—
her summer-time gaze is lucid not mild.

In the fall, I am transported to home
as I meet the chickadee-dee-dee in every province,
she fluffs out her feathers, a Canadian diamond quilt ever since
song represented Canada, from the cheerful and charming,
to her spirited patriot, still unassuming,
with a kindred eye for her brethren, she is never alone.

Part Two: An Articulate Ocean

Andromeda

I.

My existence on earth had become
more mythic than concrete:
I sat at my table, lit by a single candle,
and painstakingly embroidered
each seashell in the tapestry of the shore.
I was the sea, and the ringing
tide's familiar devotion,
its dependable crash of waters,
the spray of salt, and the wild game
of nature all embedded
themselves in my consciousness.

There was a courage to begin,
the monumental task of drawing a map
within the human soul—a diagram of life,
pertaining to freedom
from conflict, abuse, and stigma.
There was a standing,
eyes fixed, hands outstretched,
with a fury to equal the storm,
and a calling to water the shores of nations.
To be not just one
but many faces, thoughts, and emotions.

Prince George Sage

When alone, the mountain valleys
succumb to prism channels,
and undecorated, we pine
in solemn verse: this cold earth,
a primeval dome of space,
where suns and oceans meet—and now
to surface rising.

Sure souls could trade the index
of thy cavernous tide,
for rivers, streams, and hallowed countryside.

The Doorkeeper

A beryllium set in silver,
the opal in a crown:
at the head of one poor table,
a modest fare—
amongst nocturnal cavern's fire,
the dragon lair's repast.

At heart, your streams are chaliced gold
and in the underworld, we chant,
the hallowed halls bequeath
you knighthood.

The horse shall breathe his last,
in this honored battleground,
when Aurias comes stately home
and banners of the sea doth fly.

The Sea

I walked across the driftwood-littered shore
where the sea crashes with ten-year–old
impatience, wanting its mother: the moon
to dictate its moral conscience.

I am your father, said the sun,
drying the land to silt, parching the lips
of youth, and lapping at the wake of sea
in the early morning, warming the tide pools.

I am your brother, said the sand:
sleeping each night from the birds
who dig for small insects with their beaks,
and the natives who look for clams and mussels.

I am your sister, said the salt,
and you are the Sea: immersed in you,
I am forgiving of your lashing wrath
and poignant sea-star depths.

Tropical Island

The ship sailed for a distant port,
a cargo of lemon fruit and pomegranate,
the silver-white sails
weathering the sea and the storm,
the sun, a glimmering oasis
in a desert of blue.

Melody of day and night,
the monotony of raucous tune;
voyage of fortune and disguise,
the winsome rest.

The modesty of farthest star
and silken slip of moon;
the gesture of a courteous son,
planets coursing in their doom . . .

The tides of furthest fairy tale
bequeathing ocean's balm,
and lofty moments chafing wit
while palms bend to the island song.

The Wild Madonna

The sea.
Wild in its furor,
it tries to free itself
from the power which holds it;
its regulating pattern which never ceases.
It lashes the driftwood in protest
at its captivation,
flinging the logs to the shore,
then pulling them back in its undertow.
Wildly, it scatters the rocks and sand
in its path,
spraying the shore with a fine mist.

It is here that you dance,
wild like the sea,
flinging your long, coarse hair
up into the salty mist.
Dancing in your furor,
at a world condemned to die.

Linen Tablecloth

When your strong arms
find the mast, and the deck
whistles on a passage to India . . .

We are dressed in white linen
and drink lemonade,
the rough bread, coarse in our fingers,
the water, in fields of blue.

Ships pass far on the horizon,
islands come and disappear,
the great tales amuse us
long into the lantern-lit night,
the sea, a giant towering above us,
immense and staid beneath our hearth.

Altar of the Heron

The river
flowed around the island,
replenishing the banks
of fruit trees
and overhanging boughs.

The shadows swept the sun,
and salmon with gaping mouths
leapt onto the shore
in autumn, a silver
treasure of folklore.

Where once
I stood as a new bride,
decorated with beads and stones,
now my spirit daughter
meets the river
as a young woman
with long hair
and clear eyes:
laughing, clothed in
a buckskin dress
and leather sandals.

Sit on the moss,
deep in thought,
and the blue herons over the
Stave River
will guide you back
to a place of refuge.

The Traveler

Winding into the distance, the road,
speaking of the dust and foreign jewel:
travelers too-toward real abode—
a home, mended by each spool,
in the distance, never proud;
but the wanderers walk ever-on . . .
minding their thoughts, whisper prayers aloud.

I walked about to the silver sea,
I found the place where sand and briny
foam, with the horizon's cool rank, meet
fish, all sunk beneath the salt, tiny
translucent shells to adorn their graves.
Storm, now faded on the final front,
was in my navy soul's ringing naves.

Sea—forever, I in debt to thee,
destination of our homeless kind,
clearest looking-glass to somehow see
from sunrise to the end of midnight;
staid-marching to the peal of thunder,
a trumpet blast that calls us, now stand,
united as our time asunder.

House of the Sea

Queen Charlotte,
an island on the far side
of night;
constellation of stars and
mouth of the sea,
a table of plenty
beneath the harvest of moon.

The veiled echo of
England's famed cathedral:
of waves and wind,
of night sky and distant land . . .
to no longer hear
the sound
of the storm.

Part Three: Woven Ballads

Last Words From A Weaver's Basket

It's just you and me,
when the moon lies low
and the odd little winds blow,
here at our wood cabin by the sea.

It's our moment together,
when the foghorn sound fades
through deep wooded shores forever,
and the ancient ghost ships wager.

Ships would find their way
by the island's undertow.
They would 'round the bay
to the old red lighthouse's lantern glow.

The fog winds blew,
when the sky rained dew
over the tips of the woodland fir,
the weaver's basket drips with woven myrrh.

Spirit weavers stand,
as harmonic as the land—
in and out like the tide—
do the shell-brittle hands bide.

It's just you and me,
still-weaving the sea,
from the heather on the hill
to the salt-hued gulls' bill.

The rocks were rough and coarse
beneath the spirit weavers' hands,
and they were graphite bands
departing in cedar-carved force.

There was a garden for a mile
just for you and me;
sit with me for awhile,
while the lilies weave by the sea.

By the mossy shore, the ocean sighs,
where a covert cove hides,
its fingers upon the harpsichord;
resplendent is the light through the plank boards.

Wait with me for a tear
while I echo here—
spirits weaving a basket into a braid,
sit here, while I am afraid.

When there is no more sun, and no more eves,
and the earth bows down,
we will be sinking into the ground.
Sit here, while the spirit weaves.

I let you hold my hand
between sea and land,
where the pulse beats fine;
there is enough dulse for you and I.

It's just our last mussel pearl
for the sinking world,
while the wild wind blows,
and the glittering river flows.

I will not love lend,
but my fingers break and bend
with the spirit weavers, and boldly fare—
leaving behind my cold broken rocking chair.

The round wood door into paradise
lies low to the earth, but in a fever
who would unearth the gold weaver
and her basket: who would ever find it?

There is a gracious door for you and I
that we found by and by;
don't forget to listen to the brine,
and decipher her salty rhyme.

See the women on the shore there
that have turned into stones;
there is someone singing into the foam—
and the spirit weavers are braiding her hair.

Ballad of the Oboe Player

"Darling," said my mother,
winsome in the sun and rain,
"You'll need clothing of salvation,
and the seams will make me pray.

"There's nothing in my mind
that would constitute a cure for sin,
to make you autumn clothing,
to not let the winter in.

"There's nothing in my soul's lament
that could purchase hope for you,
just a molding potato, bent,
and a lettuce in the dew."

That was in Indian Summer,
then came almost winter's snow,
"Daughter, there's a legend runner
of the life before the fall crows."

Tiny little elbows, and tiny little knees,
besides the mattress bare
is rent with filth and fleas,
you're sleeping in my care.

If I had no clothes to make you
it would embarrass Mother Earth,
she would not let you run naked too,
she'd make you clothes of buckskin mirth.

When the snows had fallen glittering,
and winter had begun, fiercely beside
the icicles, were chickadees twittering,
over the clothing I had never worn outside.

In the house, I could wear velvet,
at the table, I wear pearls,
but what good is finery to catch a rabbit
and skin it for the soup of earls.

I couldn't go to school and write,
the stack of books was piled high,
like cakes I couldn't have at noon's light
or mandarins whose skins I dared not pry.

I couldn't go to church,
my shoes had holes too,
in front of all the other boys and girls
my vitamins leaked through.

Finally my mother stated, "Brawny,
I will measure you,"
and she measured every scrawny
limb, my waist and ankles too.

A tick-tock-ticking sounded
the wood grandfather clock,
busy were we, without being hounded,
yes, now we were busy with our material stock.

Busy enough not to let the wind know,
for a secret announced to the wind
is a tall tale to all upon its flaming show,
instead of the coal light of a cinder.

So here I stand, a statue girl,
in potato sacks I would relay,
whose mother could not string a pearl,
but played me music all the day.

The winter was the worst that year,
it snowed 'till March, I would wager,
the men would sit and drink a beer,
the women take a food voucher.

The snow lay to the rooftop in drifts of white,
and we melted the snow to drink water;
we cooked the last of the beans and rice,
then made soap from the olive oil to give lather.

In spring, the water with a heron's feet pooled,
and eddied in the basin,
whether your day's work was good or cruel,
there were sausages in casings.

A wolf or two howled outside the shellac
of our small wood home,
but there was nothing that we lacked
except salvation's bodice and a shell comb.

"So get out the iron," she said, "the wool,
and the cotton. Make yourself a modest girl,
who has two pigtails, bobbins, and can wear pearls.
Sew yourself a skirt by the candle's wax pool."

I saw my father sitting on the patriarchal chair,
there was newspaper for a hearth fire
that he had left in piles there;
my mother, not a moment wasted, not a tyre.

She had a porcelain doll with a little head,
and it wore green skirts, with a carol book;
she loved it and would not sell it for thread.
It was the most expensive thing we had for looks.

My father bought a clarinet at the music store,
it was made for a prince, but he gave it to me as a gift;
it made a strange sound that carried over the floor,
and my mother sat dead, and listened to my thrift.

If her fingers were saving grace, they bought my reeds;
she made attractive bead bangles,
a scarf or a hat, or sewed cilantro seeds
in a garden of flowering guardian angels.

I could play the clarinet within the band,
neat and sensible clothing belayed the olive soap,
so I memorized notes on the music stand,
and then the band master gave me an oboe.

My mother pulled the hair from the horse's tail
to stuff my mattress, made my quilt;
now we had something beyond the grail
of butter and bread, and softened guilt.

The reed resounded in the silence lonely
of the shadows, and the smiles;
we thought lovely music was like being paid in honey,
then he bought her a loom, though she was in denial.

The mourning sound had an innocuous thrill
as the loom began to fly, as the lake became the melted water,
as the oboe would play, in lilting trill,
as only a prince would wear his alma matter.

As a girl wore her salvation, sewn by her mother,
a lavender sachet in her drawer and wool stockings,
a prince was clothed in the music of the oboe,
and resplendent was its tawny mocking.

There was a lyrical pursuit that would lead,
so it seemed to a musical pauper,
but was really a poor girl with a heady reed
in one meagre song after another.

One day, I would humbly place
my instrument on my knees on the stage,
and the orchestra would pause,
as I melted souls with Gabriel's Oboe.

Part Four: New Oil

The Fragrance of Glory

A silhouette of man embroidered
his thoughts against the night:
we were waiting for heaven
in the dim blue,
and thought it good to wait,
possible to hope;
trees with their soft lips
touching the water, aqua,
again and again,
and fish swaying lazily
onward
in a fragrant world—
encompassed and vivid.
Bright like stars,
our eyes deepened,
noble and humble,
relinquishing heart
unto humanity's
gray tides
with such simplicity.

The Cottage

Soft and breathed,
silver-spun like
flaxen gold, this petal
wraps its stillness
like opals
from our eyes,
our thoughts opaque;
we thought the
baby,
dimming
beeswax, had
burned low.

Blinded, we ate poorly
in waiting and listened:
the birds cooed softly,
the night wept still,
and wrapped around my
little finger was
his hand.

Chorus

The rivulets of
streams, carrying underground
treasures, twinkled
in laughs under and over
bridges made of matchsticks.
Dressing the morning
world with silver,
they, unified, rang:
in color,
my house beneath,
filled with
the translucence
of morning's glory.

Lithograph

Once you
looked at me
in sepia from
beneath the oak,
like a man stenciled against
the sky
and whispered
a silence;
on the waterway,
footsteps of
blue and azure
tile the
staircase we climb
under
snow-fragile
stars
to heaven.

Sky Quilt

Star dreams dotted
a vivid meadow
and caressed your
head like a baby's,
nestled in a cloud,
enveloping
a patchwork kite.

I sat and made daisy chains
in the grass,
decorating the neck
of a goddess
filled with platitudes
and beatitudes,
with long hippie hair
and a bandana,
making dandelion tea.

Firebird

The dawn creased
and flew away
over the sea
like a night bird
flying
back to where the skies
bend with stars:
I watched it go
and sadly
could not miss it
as the diamonds from its
beak fell on my soft head
and left dents
and crevices
like moonbeams.

Visitor

One night
the fire kindled,
a frost blew at the door;
it opened,
and there he was—
draped from head to foot
with a glowing mantle:
back from the sky
in hues of fire
with soft delight.

Quill

Still, so
still and white
like seashells, washed
by the salt
under the weave
of ocean sounds
echoing
and sanding
the designs of man
off eternity.

Once in a dark womb,
now you write:
and the notes are
eternal black;
toe shoes,
a pirouette
on an old
pine floor.

Evening

Under the stone arches
just where the pathway
ends
and light begins,
the aurora borealis
bench
in a courtyard
of color,
foxgloves and hollyhocks
still enamored in the
evening,
one sonatina
per child:
in our enclosure,
brick by brick—
winter garden,
autumn garden,
summer garden,
spring.

Liturgy

Browned and waiting
for olive
wine that would drip and
pour, we sang
1,700 years:
and the trees echoed lightly
as wind stirs;
wounded reeds bent
at the vision,
and eloquence breathed
deeply like a burning
star,
heralded to night
in royal
velvet.

Section X: Epic Clay

still stands
in cast of burnished bronze,
and points the way
to freedom . . .

—Emily Isaacson

Part One: Revolution Song

A Catholic Star

In this dim light under a distant star,
there was a fortune to amass from bravery,
where colour distorts, exhales, and could now mar—
this people groaning 'neath the yoke of iron slavery.

Stirring my memory, bright they came:
people of heaven, not of men or same
as the desperately poor or reaching wretched,
we asked for alms from their anointed heads.

The Catholics would cast away with ease
all manner of hunger, sickness and disease,
they would stretch out a hand to your brood
of young, too many mouths and not enough food.

O joy, to receive from the higher realms:
when growing old with cares, bringing cloth bags,
my tattered highland clothing now in rags,
the crushed flowers of our souls, already used film.

This country was not endorsing hunger nor suffering
for those who had forgotten sin and mirrors.
The path to a cared-for life was not so clear;
there was an imbalance in the skies for the hurting.

The rain began to pour when they were sad,
the sun would shine its light when they were glad,
what momentary whispers of the wind's cold
would shake the poplar's gold.

Hark! My friends who stand at the gate of fear,
there is no hunger and no poverty here,
this is a refuge for your tired bodies now,
you can see the way through winter's snowy bow.

A blizzard had stopped us and we turned back,
but now we pressed forward into the black.
The future is unlike a stone olive press,
press on, and bottled at its best.

Midnight in the Street

My hands are blackened and dry,
my throat can only sing like a nightingale,
the asphalt street is quiet and stale,
so the song rings like a man's cry.

They usually say, are you a thief in the night?
Or a witch in flight?
Why does the baser world
reward you with its continuity?
Leaves swirled around the autumn
of my crystal sight,
the mist, like a death dance, twirled.

Where does my wealth accrue:
whom does the star on the horizon represent
in jewelled sparks—
the North star is lonely and dark,
she is supernal with visions,
not the medicine of pain,
nor the moon with its lesions,
this woman to evil cannot consent,
she stands alone too.

When her face is streaked with tears,
the sky lonely rains, as seers
prophesy the weather;
they are beyond your brothers,
they pick up women on street corners
only to return them to their brothel fears,
but they are what's bold and bright—
in this time beyond the sunlight.

When you can't even hear the sound
of the owl's feather,
yet it floats to earth, untethered
from the streetlight perch;
this is an underground church—
when the wind is famous and wild,
and you are its child,
somewhere loved and found.

Don't cry anymore,
don't let down your hair to the floor.

The Weeping Branch

O country of sweet sheaves, hear my humble invitation;
The branches are weeping.
There has been a struggle in the baser realms,
The virtue of the earth has been shaken.
I bring with me the spirit of Canada,
A pleading to your noble station.

The world has seen your heart despised.
I spoke to you and you replied.
When I sing of revolution in the dead of night,
  you hear.
Then answer me with all your might.

This is the moment of the turning,
  and it is not for the weak;
Much is at stake.
I prophesied the sanguine salt was guileless,
And chunks of coal were your revenge in darkness.
The oyster sun spoke over the sea,
Churning the machinery of democracy.

O Canada:
I was born into the quiet moments of Windsor,
I am a prophet under the order of Samuel.
Canada's gates will never be shut;
I am last to call my people home.
I am in it 'till the bitter end.

Part Two: Flaming Beginnings

Old Majestic Trees

Hope gave way, plummeted far below
where Tolerance could not wield a sword,
and Joy not soothe, Mercy could not go.
Humility was a runner toward
the ribbon prize, the far final goal,
and where I lagged behind, I now found
renewed reverence without old toll.

The blind that stumble shall see again
finding their way through that vast dark night,
lit by stars eternal, that began
flaming at the birth of time, when flight
took each bird to try his dampened wing,
and Mercy rested upon the branch
of old majestic trees, ages sing.

The deaf shall hear, and are now relieved
that beyond Hope, Mercy speaks today:
a generous hymn and they believed
that all good fortune would come their way,
the blisters of the lonesome path, healed;
woman stands shaded in the doorway—
the sober love of sacred heart, sealed.

Sonnet IX

Do not in stagnant water flow, but swim
in the river with clear springs—at the brim
of sunlight's last clean sweep of sky, as lone
as the moons of Saturn, hung one by one
in your Creator hands, turn brevity
to song and valor emanates from this:
that the mind is theologically
inclined to do war and battles forthwith.
Take out one's sword, and triumph!—slay the foe
at this last hour, when earth is falling low;
into a field, death's horse now circles round
and ends the rider's life on gravestone mound.
What richness would this world to all direct,
that in its bosom, neither could protect.

The Altar

You are the altar
on which I am sacrificed on rough stones,
praying like a bird in a cage,
steeling my forehead as a farmer does
when his plough must go forward,
seeing the sun drop in the sky.

And the clouds ever-move,
sculpted by the master.
Drifting from one thought
to the next, composed.

The rain falls, on dormant
worlds and high-strung gardens.
A cellist sits on the wall
and plays toward evening.

You are the womb of life
and when I am born I am firmly in your grasp.
Holding me to the breast
is the mother of life,
and the breath in me must go forward . . .
'till death lays me in a field.

Part Three: Ancient Dreams

The Apothecary's Daughter

At the apothecary shop
is the crossroads of medieval medicine,
where change is of the essence,
and time stands alone.

She is young, she is strong with laughter,
and her will is steady;
her hazel eyes speak of healing
her lips are a rose, speaking in the wind,
her hands are as skillful as the land,
the tonic bends beneath her hands,
vials and ointments
are scepters extended to the poor and ill:
she is the apothecary's daughter.

Carnelian—
her face is flax damask,
as she travels with a cowl over her head
through the cloister's silence dead,
she carries the crude anthracite
to her father's benefactor's rite.

The children play in burgundy knickers
around the fountain,
but she is as silent as dawn
and threading doves,
as the far-away gallop of hooves
on a crusade.

"I can turn a thistle to a daffodil in a day,"
said the passing alchemist
with a wry smile,
"and the rain becomes
crystals beneath my hand.
My skull is made of wood, not clay."

"What creates the connection
between the roses
are the thorns,"
said the apothecary's daughter.
"For you are an illusionist,
and I am Carnelian,
the thorn of perdition."

"Hold it to your lantern glass,
for you are a rose—
(I do not want the roses to be without
stems or leaves or thorns . . .)"
said the alchemist.
"Through the glass is a light,
and beneath my heart
there is a country—
you have found the Door!"

"Alas," she paused,
"if there is a country within you,
there is an empire
within me—"

"What empire? Apothecary's daughter,"
he asked with a jeer,
"What empire protects you?"

"Why it is the empire of the royal rose,"
she stood her ground.
He looked through his spectacle at her closely:
"The royal rose that entwines the golden arbour—
is that the empire of which you speak?"

"It is an aged rose
from which steeps
the sweet perfume of roses' oil,
as I would know,"
she answered.
"Then be assured
that I not only
know the secret of the rose,
but the place from which it sprang—
that would make a maiden weep."

"I weep as surely
as I live, if I do not know
the medicine of the gorse, the heather,
and of the rose:
it springs from
the rose hip,
and is a woman's remedy.
Now, I must be off,
for my smokeless coal
is growing dim
before my eyes—" she said.

Aha! thought the alchemist—
the lady did not know that
we would meet,
for until now I could only dream
of her medicine
to make a woman sweet.

The arched passage rang
with his voice,
for he scarce cared to lower it.
"Your father knows both
his friends and benefactors,"
he said, "but does he know his enemies?"

"Pray tell, who is his enemy?"
she asked. "There is a robin perched
on his chestnut bud."
"Why his enemy is anyone who,
with skill, is cunning
and works to undermine him," he said.
"What is within the human heart, will
eventually flower after its own kind,
for it cannot stay hidden very long.

"If, a dance," he said, taking her hand,
"it must be worked out
as a sequence of steps,
while dripping with sweat."

"The life without it, though,
is passionless," she said.

"Toil in the valleys
of the human heart
for happiness is hard to find,
and when we find it
we let go all too soon.

"We breathe and spin
and leap—our faith in our mouths,
our life lived with one last
mournful cry," he said.

They had met at last—
a chance meeting:
"And what is your name?" she asked.
"Waterford," he answered.

"Waterford, the son of crusaders?" she asked.
"Yes, and keeper of the Waterford Journal—
for I can write," he said.
"You may not remember me,
but I was in your benefactor's school
as a child. Do you remember I sent you a note?"

"Aye," said Carnelian, "but I could not read it."

"I will tell you what it said," he answered.

"Do not despise thou love, nor rue its share,
the shelter it provides is providence,
the elegance of home is free from cares,
and thine bent head in prayer is evidence.
I have many flowers in my garden,
each smells so sweetly of the summer's air,
envelopes of color, secret wardens,
for all the trust that heav'n keeps guarded there.
If ever I should give my heart to one,
I would find her 'neath an arbour waiting;
my intimations second to her none,
there'd be one song in my mouth abating:
I would give thee my youth's flattery now
that I may not prove false upon thy vow."

"I remember now," said Carnelian.
"Then you were last to read it," he said.

"Last was I to read your cream folded note,
when I was still quite young, I would not laugh
at your sincerity, and my wood staff.
My reputation was my ivory throat.
I would take you at your word, upon sea
I float: saline is my buffer, salt pure
that reaches deep into my wounds, censured
as crystalline mine salt, deep in the green,
we move, we float, licensed liquidity.
And now the years have almost passed me by,
I remember you, the boy that once kythed
in books and music, gardens' flow'r to me.
Do not let me forget the passing age,
that once held me, a player, on the stage."

Part Four: Maid of Orleans

Portal of the North Wind

Under the open scepter,
chancellor a sepulchral undertone,
I fledged my wings to fly by night,
and took the westward course.

In foul caverns, goblins dwell,
the ghouls of time will shed their souls,
and hags entice the fledgling knight
who knelt in sunny palace once.

The ladies' bed, a veiled forgery,
some royal velvet cue abandoned,
a once-shed tear from Christmas night
and holly boughs will glow
with solstice.

O angel of ye gods,
who stands at tiptoe's reach:
relinquishment, your sword of peace.

The refuge of thine arms,
an unaccounted piece now played;
we wallowed lowly once
to reach thy vestal eternal throne.

Corvus

I.

The bold stems
and the clear perfume of the Maid of Orleans,
fill an apron with sweet tender petals,
the perfect flower of the conservatory,
reveling in the hush of amazement
subtle as the voices of angels,
the feathering of wings surrounding
a high-strung temperament without languor,
the mission whispered
in hushed tones to a priest,
both of unity and dissonance.

The barely discernible canon
was an eclipse between sun and moon,
a truce when her disquisition
showed its allegiance
leading to her confinement and restraint
as the sea within its bounds;
the maid prayed to God.
Fervent, she leapt from the tower,
escaping with no malice,
with a widow's peak in her forehead
until the nation stood at the gates of unrequited love.

Unchained Love

I will . . .
I will be yours.
I will laugh with you
and tell stories beneath the stars,
and bury children in the leaves
with you.

I will climb the old apple tree
in the orchard with you,
I will gather shells along the shore
in summer,
and drink cider by the fire
in winter,
with you.

I will mend missing buttons,
and kiss tender tears
and hope for happiness
through the years,
because I love you.

A Mission

I look into your eyes,
the playwright of times,
and in their sincere depths
taste the purity of love.

Only the one enamored prince of time
came on a gallant midnight steed,
through milky universe and earth,
to radiant countrymen and
white-clothed bride.

Immortality

Your sword is silver,
and your speech is clean—
I taste the moment of truth.

Cloistered in the inner chamber
behind the wrought iron gate,
sitting on the hard bench,
with Latin voices
mingling in the hallway:

Now for hours
I presume
to be a dying Christ,
without a motion,
without thought,
I stretch and die
under the crucifix,
on the cold stone floor,
hang on a cross—

Immortality.

My heart is
and always shall
be yours.

Emerging Sparrows and Salt

A sparrow flew out over the rooftops—
a small creature, unseen,
yet a small girl opened her window—
and wished the bird godspeed.

If there were two bags of salt,
two witnesses,
now there are many—
in nascent culpability
to define good and evil
in the light of community.
The salt dispersed over the ice.

Wherever a sparrow emerges
and flies,
do we remember her still?

Endnotes

Opening quotes

William Shakespeare, *The Complete Works of William Shakespeare: The Cambridge Text.* (Galley Press: W.H Smith and Son Ltd., 1982). Macbeth. Act. IV. Scene III. 37-41. General domain.

"reception": The Door. Emily Isaacson, *The Fleur-de-lis Vol I* (Tate Publishing & Enterprises, 2011), 29.

Section I: Stand at the Window

Part One: Dogwood Manor

Threnody of the Thistle p.5. Emily Isaacson, *Victoriana* (Tate Publishing & Enterprises, 2015), 25.

Woman Prophet p.6. Emily Isaacson, *The Fleur-de-lis, Vol III* (Tate Publishing & Enterprises, 2011), 150.

Where I Found Her p.7. Emily Isaacson, *The Fleur-de-lis, Vol III* (Tate Publishing & Enterprises, 2011), 151.

Spiritual Touch p.8-9. Emily Isaacson, *The Fleur-de-lis, Vol III* (Tate Publishing & Enterprises), 95-96.

Section II: Mottled Recession

Part One: Layered Realism

Apples of Gold in Settings of Silver p.33. Emily Isaacson, *O Canada: Celebrating 150 Years* (Fraser Valley Poets' Society, 2017), 107.

View of Mount Song p.36. Emily Isaacson, *O Canada: Celebrating 150 Years* (Fraser Valley Poets' Society, 2017) (as "The Waterford Journal"), 139.

In the Custody of Angels p.37. Emily Isaacson, *O Canada: Celebrating 150 Years* (Fraser Valley Poets' Society), 167.

Part Two: Spare Minimalism

Beside the Golden Door p.40. Quote: Emma Lazarus, 1883, from the Statue of Liberty. Emily Isaacson, *O Canada: Celebrating 150 Years* (Fraser Valley Poets' Society, 2017), 93

A Street of Many Doors p.42. Emily Isaacson. *O Canada: Celebrating 150 Years* (Fraser Valley Poets' Society, 2017), 29.

A House of Many Walls p.44 (adapted version). Emily Isaacson, *O Canada: Celebrating 150 Years* (Fraser Valley Poets' Society 2017), 73.

Part Three: Gothic Architecture

The Peace Tower p.52. Emily Isaacson, *The Fleur-de-lis, Vol III* (Tate Publishing & Enterprises, 2011), 177.

The Little Match Girl p.53. Emily Isaacson, *O Canada: Celebrating 150 Years* (Fraser Valley Poets' Society, 2017), 76

Anna Pavlova p.54. Emily Isaacson, *The Fleur-de-lis, Vol II, Set V.* (Tate Publishing & Enterprises, 2011), 163.

Ara p.55. Emily Isaacson, *A Familiar Shore* (Tate Publishing & Enterprises, 2015) poem I., 42.

Bootes p.57. Emily Isaacson, *A Familiar Shore* (Tate Publishing & Enterprises, 2015) poem I., 54.

Braithwaite p.58-59. Emily Isaacson, *The Fleur-de-lis, Vol II* (Tate Publishing & Enterprises, 2017), 15-16.

Dorado p.60. Emily Isaacson, *A Familiar Shore* (Tate Publishing & Enterprises, 2015), poem I., 152

The Writer's Neck of the Woods p.61. Emily Isaacson, *House of Rain* (Potter's Press, 2013), 44.

Gemini p.62. Emily Isaacson, *A Familiar Shore* (Tate Publishing & Enterprises, 2015), poem I., 172. Theme poem for grass-roots movement *One Million Burning*, also published at www.onemillionburning.com.

Part Four: The Enamoured Romantic

Ace p.64. Emily Isaacson, *The Fleur-de-lis, Vol III* (Tate Publishing & Enterprises, 2011), poem I., 345

Remnant p.65. Emily Isaacson, *The Fleur-de-lis, Vol III* (Tate Publishing & Enterprises, 2011), "The Poet Edward; Dance of the Bards X.", 200.

One Still Fertile Field p.66-67. Emily Isaacson, *The Fleur-de-lis, Vol II* (Tate Publishing & Enterprises, 2011), 206-207.

The Muse p.68. Emily Isaacson, *House of Rain* (Potter's Press, 2013), 18.

Aria: Togetsukyo Bridge p.69. Emily Isaacson, *The Fleur-de-lis, Vol II* (Tate Publishing & Enterprises, 2011), 209.

The Ship Lantern p.70-71. Emily Isaacson, *The Fleur-de-lis, Vol III* (Tate Publishing & Enterprises, 2011), 363-364.

Constellation p.72. Emily Isaacson, *The Fleur-de-lis, Vol I* (Tate Publishing & Enterprises, 2011), 104.

Tryst p.73. Emily Isaacson, *The Fleur-de-lis, Vol III* (Tate Publishing & Enterprises, 2011), p. 366.

On Browning Boughs p.74. Emily Isaacson, *House of Rain* (Potter's Press, 2013), 60.

Of Foreign Lands and People p.75. Emily Isaacson, *The Fleur-de-lis, Vol III* (Tate Publishing & Enterprises, 2011), "Poverty V.", 413. Title from a classical music piece by Robert Schumann.

Section III: Contemplative Design

Part Three: Signature Heartfelt Style

Mother Contemplation p.104. Emily Isaacson, *City of Roses* (Potter's Press, 2015), 80.

Father Contemplation p.105. Emily Isaacson, *City of Roses* (Potter's Press, 2015), 129.

Elder Contemplation p.106. Emily Isaacson, *City of Roses* (Potter's Press, 2015), 199.

Ancient of Days Contemplation p.107. Emily Isaacson, *City of Roses* (Potter's Press, 2015), 158.

Daughter Contemplation p.108. Emily Isaacson, *City of Roses* (Potter's Press, 2015), 246.

Son Contemplation p.109. Emily Isaacson, *City of Roses* (Potter's Press, 2015), 182.

Child Contemplation p.110. Emily Isaacson, *City of Roses* (Potter's Press, 2015), 44.

Hero Contemplation p.111. Emily Isaacson, *City of Roses* (Potter's Press, 2015), 223.

Physician Contemplation p.112. Emily Isaacson, *City of Roses* (Potter's Press, 2015), 271.

Divine Contemplation p.113. Emily Isaacson, *City of Roses* (Potter's Press, 2015), 307.

Friend Contemplation p.114. Emily Isaacson, *City of Roses* (Potter's Press, 2015), 340.

Presence Contemplation p.115. Emily Isaacson, *City of Roses* (Potter's Press, 2015), 355.

River Contemplation p.116. Emily Isaacson, *City of Roses* (Potter's Press, 2015), 110.

Section IV: Circle Keeping

Part Three: Native Land

The Loom of the North p.136. Emily Isaacson, *The Fleur-de-lis, Vol I* (Tate Publishing & Enterprises, 2011), 42.

Wilderness   p.137. Emily Isaacson, *The Fleur-de-lis, Vol I* (Tate Publishing & Enterprises, 2011), 46.

House of the Snow p.138. Emily Isaacson, *The Fleur-de-lis, Vol I* (Tate Publishing & Enterprises, 2011), 51

River Cabin p.139. Emily Isaacson, *The Fleur-de-lis, Vol I* (Tate Publishing & Enterprises, 2011), 60.

Portrait p.140. Emily Isaacson, *The Fleur-de-lis, Vol I* (Tate Publishing & Enterprises, 2011), 68.

New Moon p.141. Emily Isaacson, *The Fleur-de-lis, Vol I* (Tate Publishing & Enterprises, 2011), 70.

Star of the Sea Art Gallery p.142. Emily Isaacson, *The Fleur-de-lis, Vol I* (Tate Publishing & Enterprises, 2011), 72.

Rockies p.143. Emily Isaacson, *The Fleur-de-lis, Vol* I (Tate Publishing & Enterprises, 2011), 94.

Bridle Of The North p.144. Emily Isaacson, *The Fleur-de-lis, Vol I* (Tate Publishing & Enterprises, 2011), 105.

O Immortal p.145. Emily Isaacson, *The Fleur-de-lis, Vol I* (Tate Publishing & Enterprises, 2011), 109.

Section V: A Handful of Sonnets

Part One: Winsome Nostalgia

Soldier-like, bravest man a rising moon— p.159. Eclipsed poem inspired by Victor's Hugo's play "Hernani." *The Works of Victor Hugo: One Volume Edition.* (Walter J. Black, Inc., 1928), 777.

Part Two: Bergamot Brocade

A voice cries out, I dare not turn my head, p.163. Eclipsed poem inspired by Victor's Hugo's play "Hernani." *The Works of Victor Hugo: One Volume Edition.* (Walter J. Black, Inc., 1928), 777.

I am an agent blind of all sadness, p.169. Eclipsed poem inspired by Victor's Hugo's play "Hernani." *The Works of Victor Hugo: One Volume Edition.* (Walter J. Black, Inc., 1928), 777.

Part Three: Classic Shades

When you retreat alone into the wood, p.177. Eclipsed poem inspired by Victor's Hugo's play "Hernani." *The Works of Victor Hugo: One Volume Edition.* (Walter J. Black, Inc., 1928), 777.

Section IX: Postmodern Poems

Part One: Canadian Eclectic

Grey Jay p.252. This bird was selected by National Geographic as Canada's National Bird this year (2017). The four runner ups were also the subject of these five bird poems, and the material used to write them were the thousands of comments by voters on the National Geographic website. Thank you to all the Canadians who participated and made these poems a work of art on behalf of all contributors.

Part Two: An Articulate Ocean

Andromeda p.258. Emily Isaacson, *A Familiar Shore* (Tate Publishing & Enterprises, 2015), poem II., 23.

Prince George Sage p.259. Emily Isaacson, *The Fleur-de-lis, Vol III* (Tate Publishing & Enterprises, 2011), 377.

The Doorkeeper p.260. Emily Isaacson, *The Fleur-de-lis, Vol II* (Tate Publishing & Enterprises, 2011), 83.

The Sea p.261. Emily Isaacson, *House of Rain* (Potter's Press, 2013), 46.

Tropical Island p.262. Emily Isaacson, *The Fleur-de-lis, Vol III* (Tate publishing & Enterprises, 2011), 362.

The Wild Madonna p.263. Emily Isaacson, *The Fleur-de-lis, Vol II* (Tate Publishing & Enterprises, 2011), 215.

Linen Tablecloth p.264. Emily Isaacson, *The Fleur-de-lis, Vol III* (Tate Publishing & Enterprises, 2011), 383.

Altar of the Heron p.265. Emily Isaacson, *The Fleur-de-lis, Vol II* (Tate Publishing & Enterprises, 2011), 189.

The Traveler p.266. Emily Isaacson, *House of Rain,* (Potter's Press, 2013), 51.

House of the Sea p.267. Emily Isaacson, *The Fleur-de-lis, Vol I* (Tate Publishing & Enterprises, 2011), 63

Part Four: New Oil

The Fragrance of Glory p.280. Emily Isaacson, *The Fleur-de-lis, Vol I* (Tate Publishing & Enterprises, 2011), 270.

The Cottage p.281. Emily Isaacson, *The Fleur-de-lis, Vol I* (Tate Publishing & Enterprises, 2011), 180.

Chorus p.282. Emily Isaacson, *The Fleur-de-lis, Vol I* (Tate Publishing & Enterprises, 2011), 182.

Lithograph p.283. Emily Isaacson, *The Fleur-de-lis, Vol I* (Tate Publishing & Enterprises, 2011), 183.

Sky Quilt p.284. Emily Isaacson, *The Fleur-de-lis, Vol I* (Tate Publishing & Enterprises, 2011), 184.

Firebird p.285. Emily Isaacson, *The Fleur-de-lis, Vol I* (Tate Publishing & Enterprises, 2011), 185.

Visitor p.286. Emily Isaacson, *The Fleur-de-lis, Vol I* (Tate Publishing & Enterprises, 2011), 186.

Quill p.287. Emily Isaacson, *The Fleur-de-lis, Vol I* (Tate Publishing & Enterprises, 2011), 187.

Evening p.288. Emily Isaacson, *The Fleur-de-lis, Vol I* (Tate Publishing & Enterprises, 2011), 188.

Liturgy p.289. Emily Isaacson, *The Fleur-de-lis, Vol I* (Tate Publishing & Enterprises, 2011), 189.

Section X: Epic Clay

Part One: Revolution Song

The Weeping Branch p.298. Emily Isaacson, *O Canada: Celebrating 150 Years* (Fraser Valley Poet's Society, 2017), 51.

Part Two: Flaming Beginnings

Old Majestic Trees p.300. Emily Isaacson, *House of Rain* (Potter's Press, 2013), 26.

Sonnet IX p.301. Emily Isaacson, *House of Rain* (Potter's Press, 2013), 41.

The Altar p.302. Emily Isaacson, *House of Rain* (Potter's Press, 2013), 106.

Part Four: Maid of Orleans

Portal of the North Wind p.312. Emily Isaacson, *The Fleur-de-lis, Vol II* (Tate Publishing & Enterprises, 2011), 109.

Corvus p.313. Emily Isaacson, *A Familiar Shore* (Tate Publishing & Enterprises, 2015), poem I., 132.

Unchained Love p.314. Emily Isaacson, *The Fleur-de-lis, Vol III* (Tate Publishing & Enterprises, 2011) titled "Poverty III," 417.

A Mission (orig. Immortality VII.) and Immortality (orig. Immortality VIII.) p.315-316. Emily Isaacson, *The Fleur-de-lis, Vol III* (Tate Publishing & Enterprises, 2011), 422-423.

~

All section quotes from Oracle of the Stone; Emily Isaacson, *The Fleur-de-lis, Vol II* (Tate Publishing & Enterprises, 2011), 195-219.

57451676R00207

Made in the USA
Columbia, SC
09 May 2019